Teach One Another
Words of Wisdom

Selections from the
Religious Educator

Edited by Richard Neitzel Holzapfel and David M. Whitchurch

RELIGIOUS STUDIES CENTER
BRIGHAM YOUNG UNIVERSITY

RELIGIOUS STUDIES CENTER
BRIGHAM YOUNG UNIVERSITY

Published by the Religious Studies Center, Brigham Young University, Provo, Utah
http://religion.byu.edu/rsc_rec_pub.php

© 2009 by Brigham Young University
All rights reserved

Printed in the United States of America by Sheridan Books, Inc.

Any uses of this material beyond those allowed by the exemptions in U.S. copyright law, such as section 107, "Fair Use," and section 108, "Library Copying," require the written permission of the publisher, Religious Studies Center, 167 HGB, Brigham Young University, Provo, Utah 84602. The views expressed herein are the responsibility of the authors and do not necessarily represent the position of Brigham Young University or the Religious Studies Center.

ISBN 978-0-8425-2717-0
Retail U.S. $8.95

Cover photo © courtesy of Mark Karrass/Corbis
Cover design by Kristin Call

Table of Contents

v   Introduction
       Richard Neitzel Holzapfel and David M. Whitchurch

1   The Journey of Lifelong Learning
       Elder Robert D. Hales

15   To Learn and to Teach More Effectively
       Elder Richard G. Scott

29   Teaching the Atonement
       Elder Tad R. Callister

43   Ever Learning, Ever Teaching:
       Lessons from Joseph F. Smith
       David M. Whitchurch

73   Christmas and Childhood
       J. R. Kearl

85   "Those Who See":
       A Century's Charge to Religious Educators
       Scott C. Esplin and Brent R. Esplin

111   How to Ask Questions That Invite Revelation
       Alan R. Maynes

123   Effective Classroom Time Management
       Scott H. Knecht

127   Raising the Bar: Preparing Future Missionaries
       Brent L. Top

145   Helping Children to Be Lifelong Learners
       Don and Ann Pearson

161   On Getting Engaged
       Kathy Kipp Clayton

169   "Tap Lightly": Managing Classroom Behavior
       William C. Ostenson

175   Index

For ten years, the *Religious Educator* has provided a venue for scholars and students of the Restoration to explore Church history, ancient and modern scripture and doctrine, and approaches in understanding and teaching the principles of the gospel of Jesus Christ.

Photo by Richard B. Crookston

Introduction

Richard Neitzel Holzapfel and David M. Whitchurch

Jeffrey R. Holland, then dean of Religious Instruction at Brigham Young University (BYU), established the Religious Studies Center (RSC) in 1975 with the mission of encouraging and supporting the pursuit of truth through scholarship on gospel-related topics. This collection of essays, like all RSC endeavors, is part of Religious Education's overall mission of building the kingdom of God by teaching and preserving the sacred doctrine and history of the gospel of Jesus Christ.

When Robert L. Millet, then dean of Religious Education at BYU, initiated the publication of the *Religious Educator* (*TRE*) in 2000, he wanted to provide another venue for scholars and students of the Restoration to explore our rich Church history, plumb the depths of ancient and modern scripture and doctrine, and highlight approaches in understanding and teaching the principles of the gospel of Jesus Christ.

During the ten years of its history, *TRE* has been a place where dedicated Church leaders and seasoned teachers could publish thoughtful, well-researched essays and articles that highlight how to teach important and timely gospel principles. The collective volumes provide a remarkable library of pedagogical and devotional resources that have and will bless and inspire the lives of its many readers.

This, the tenth year of *TRE*, provides an ideal and timely opportunity to bring together two special volumes of some of the best articles and essays from past issues—one devoted to doctrinal and historical subjects, and the other dedicated to gospel teaching. The few articles included in this volume are just a small sampling from the numerous articles published over the past decade. We believe they typify meaningful and efficacious teaching. May they be a blessing to all who read and apply the principles to their own teaching.

Elder Hales's devotional address "The Journey of Lifelong Learning" was given on August 19, 2008, during Campus Education Week.

The Journey of Lifelong Learning

Elder Robert D. Hales

Elder Robert D. Hales *is a member of the Quorum of the Twelve Apostles.*

This devotional address was given on August 19, 2008, during Campus Education Week.

Today in this devotional I am honored to be addressing those committed to lifelong learning.

Our quest for knowledge and our journey of eternal progression began long before our mortal existence. We are given a clear understanding that during the Council in Heaven we used our agency, choosing to come to earth and participate in mortality. In choosing to come to this earth, we were choosing the opportunity to progress, to grow, and to gain more knowledge. And in that process of learning and coming to earth, taking upon us a mortal body to gain knowledge and to experience mortality is an essential part of our eternal learning and progression.

The theme of lifelong learning is important because for Latter-day Saints the lifelong pursuit of knowledge is not only secular but spiritual. We understand that gaining knowledge is essential to gaining eternal salvation. Brigham Young said, "Should our lives be extended to a thousand years, still we may live and learn."[1]

For most worldly and temporal possessions, the old adage is true: You can't take it with you. However, the intellectual treasures of knowledge and spiritual values hold a promise of eternal significance. We read in the Doctrine and Covenants, "Whatever principle of intelligence we attain unto in this life, it will rise with us in the resurrection. And if a person gains more knowledge and intelligence in this life through his diligence and obedience than another, he will have so much the advantage in the world to come" (D&C 130:18–19).

So while mortality is only a small moment in eternity, learning throughout our mortal lives is an essential part of our eternal education. Here on earth, as Brigham Young once observed, "we are in a great school."[2]

When we see our learning here as part of our eternal education, we raise our sights for learning. As children, we might have begun learning because our parents coaxed or cajoled us. They wanted us to acquire a formal education with college degrees or technical labor skills, knowing that at the end of our labors we would be rewarded by being self-sufficient, productive, and able to survive in the real world. Some of us studied hard as we became interested in the stiff competition for grades and honors.

While these motivations for learning played important roles at different times in our lives, if they are our only motivations, we will stop learning when our parents or teachers are gone and our degrees are earned. Lifelong learners are driven by more eternal motives. One of the giant steps in maturing and acquiring knowledge and experience is when we learn for the joy of being edified rather than for the pleasure of being entertained. The goal of the wisest lifelong learners is not so much to impress others but to improve themselves and to help others. Their desire is to learn and to change their behavior by following the sound counsel and example imparted from great teachers around them.

Sometimes our learning is limited if we think of it as only one course at a time or getting one degree. But as we look to the scriptures, they give us the curriculum of the lifetime learner: "Things both in heaven and in the earth, and under the earth; things which have been, things which are, things which must shortly come to pass; things which are at home, things which are abroad; the wars and the perplexities of the nations, and the judgments which are on the land; and a knowledge also of countries and of kingdoms" (D&C 88:79).

The first verse of the Book of Mormon reads, "I, Nephi, having been born of goodly parents, therefore I was taught somewhat in all the learning of my father" (1 Nephi 1:1). Just as Nephi's field of study was all that his father knew, lifelong learners know no disciplinary boundaries in their quest for greater knowledge.

Lifelong learners have an insatiable inner desire to acquire knowledge in a broad range of subjects and disciplines. Thus the reward for lifelong learners is simply the joy of learning and acquiring knowledge in a wide spectrum of subjects that interest them.

Some may wonder whether it is possible to teach lifelong learning or if it is simply a genetic gift. Just as some are born with greater speed, some of us may naturally have a greater desire for learning. Yet just as wise coaches can improve anyone willing to pay the price, in like manner Heavenly Father is eager to bless us with the drive and determination to become lifelong learners if we are willing to pay the price.

Oftentimes it takes a great teacher to motivate us and to instill that desire in us. How can we improve our desire and increase the desire of others to gain more knowledge over a lifetime of learning experiences?

Attributes of Lifelong Learners

It is important to consider the attributes that one must acquire to become a lifelong learner. A few of the basic attributes needed to become a lifelong learner are courage, faithful desire, humility, patience, curiosity, and a willingness to communicate and share the knowledge that we gain. Let's take a moment to pause and reflect in more depth how each of these attributes may contribute to our becoming a lifelong learner. And the other side of the coin would be to consider how we may be able to instill lifelong learning in those around us, especially our children.

Courage. "Be of good courage, and he shall strengthen your heart, all ye that hope in the Lord" (Psalm 31:24).

Lifelong learners have the courage to overcome the fear of leaving the outer limits of their educational comfort zone and entering into the unknown and the unfamiliar. The scriptures say, "For God hath not given us the spirit of fear; but of power, and of love, and of a sound mind" (2 Timothy 1:7).

Too often we dwell in the comfort of our educational strengths and avoid overcoming our educational weaknesses. Thus our greatest strengths can become our greatest weaknesses. We may dwell in the security of the past, unwilling to venture into the future because of the fear of ignorance or the lack of knowledge about a subject we desire to study or to research. We need the courage to take a long step of faith into a fearful darkness, not knowing how deep the educational cave is that we are about to enter.

Fear is only dispelled by the amount of intellectual light we are willing to shine on the dark educational abyss that is a void in our understanding. We must find the courage to go forward—to press on. We read in the Doctrine and Covenants, "There were fears in your hearts, and verily this is the reason that ye did not receive" (D&C 67:3). Despite our fears, courage in acquiring new learning is essential for lifelong learners.

Faithful desire. "Seek ye diligently and teach one another words of wisdom; yea, seek ye out of the best books words of wisdom; seek learning, even by study and also by faith" (D&C 88:118).

Next is faithful desire. Lifelong learners have an insatiable, unselfish inner desire to acquire a wide spectrum of knowledge across many disciplines for the mere joy of attaining and sharing the increased knowledge without any recognition or rewards. Oftentimes the motivation and desire for learning is stimulated by a perceived need to help others. For example, a concerned mother who feels there is a lack of a medical diagnosis concerning a family physical or mental health problem researches medical books and journals to assist in the solution.

A lifelong learner may have a desire for self-improvement to have a happier or more benevolent life. Lifelong learners have a desire for knowledge that will help them to be better helpmeets, better mothers, better fathers, better citizens, and better servants in the Lord's kingdom so "that [they] may learn and glorify the name of [their] God" (2 Nephi 6:4).

Humility. "Let him that is ignorant learn wisdom by humbling himself and calling upon the Lord his God, that his eyes may be opened that he may see, and his ears opened that he may hear" (D&C 136:32).

Next is the quality of humility. Lifelong learners recognize the source of all knowledge is a gift from God. "He that truly humbleth himself . . . , the same shall be blessed" (Alma 32:15).

Because lifelong learners recognize that intelligence is a gift of God, they do not dwell on it or become prideful about their personal intelligence quotient or accomplishments. Each new discovery of knowledge is metered out from on high in the Lord's time and in the Lord's way "line upon line, precept upon precept" (2 Nephi 28:30).

When we are truly humble, we remember that knowledge and wisdom are given to us by the Lord and that we are to use that knowledge and wisdom in lifting and strengthening others: "To every man is given a gift by the Spirit of God. To some is given one, and to some is given another, that all may be profited thereby" (D&C 46:11–12). We gain knowledge to better serve.

Patience. "Add to your faith virtue; and to virtue knowledge; and to knowledge temperance; and to temperance patience; and to patience godliness" (2 Peter 1:5–6).

Lifelong learners acquire an inordinate degree of patience in their quest for learning. They understand through their diligent search for learning that it takes a great deal of energy and a great deal of time to find pure knowledge.

What a feeling! Have you ever sought for something—searched, pondered, and prayed—until *finally* there it was, right before you? Sometimes what we learn today may not seem valuable until months or even years into the future. We not only learn but we ponder that knowledge so that in the right place, at the right time, we can put it to the best use.

Curiosity. "I applied mine heart to know, and to search, and to seek out wisdom, and the reason of things" (Ecclesiastes 7:25).

The next quality is curiosity. My sister used to say to me, "Curiosity killed the cat, but satisfaction brought him back."

Lifelong learners are curious at heart. As children, our curiosity is instinctive, but our formal education is more confining and systematic. Lifelong learners develop personalized learning techniques that surpass what is taught in school. The key learning element is that they never lose their God-given inherent curiosity. They are simply detectives or sleuths in the image of Sherlock Holmes, solving a case by putting together the facts that they have gathered. They do it by asking the question "why" and then finding the answers. The thrill of investigating and researching a new concept or discovering the answer to something previously unknown to us is an exhilarating moment of joy and satisfaction.

Lifelong learners learn "line upon line" and "precept upon precept" but also have personal "aha" moments when they see all at once the larger picture. The lifelong learner does not give up. Thomas Edison was a lifelong learner. He was attributed as saying, "I have not failed, I've just found ten thousand ways that won't work."

Communication. "Wherefore, he that preacheth and he that receiveth, understand one another, and both are edified and rejoice together" (D&C 50:22).

Lifelong learners are teachers at heart, reveling in the communication of learning and knowledge. They find joy when those whom they teach by sharing their knowledge are uplifted and strengthened. They communicate with God through prayer for guidance and knowledge. They communicate with God to give thanks and gratitude for the knowledge they have received. They communicate with other lifelong learners, listening intensively in a two-way exchange of learning that is mutually beneficial to all.

Great teachers are not only great communicators but also great listeners. When we are communicating, we can learn something from every individual we meet.

Great teachers produce lifelong learners. Great teachers do not provide all the answers to their students. They lead them to the fountain of knowledge and instill in them a desire to drink. Great teachers motivate students to seek knowledge.

One educator was in a meeting with President Packer in a question-and-answer period. President Packer was asked about his teachings on the Atonement. What did he teach? They wanted a testimony and a full dissertation from him on the Atonement. That's what they expected from this great teacher. His answer taught everyone there about lifelong learning. President Packer replied, "Read the Book of Mormon a few times, searching for teachings about the Atonement. Then write a one-page summary of what you have learned. Then, my dear brother, you will have your answer."

Scripture Study and Lifelong Learning

Scripture study is a lifelong learning experience. Perhaps nowhere can we see the need for lifelong learning more clearly than with scripture study. No matter how many times we may read the scriptures, through the power and inspiration of the Holy Ghost we learn new truths and gain valuable counsel and insights to meet life's challenges. President Ezra Taft Benson taught, "Yesterday's meal is not enough to sustain today's needs. So also an infrequent reading of [the Book of Mormon,] 'the most correct of any book on earth,' as Joseph Smith called it, is not enough."[3]

The primary purposes of scripture study are to gain gospel understanding and to strengthen us spiritually. One reason we need to continually feast on the words of Christ is that, like all learning, gospel understanding and spiritual insights come one precept at a time.

Scripture study is a unique form of learning. It requires literacy—the ability to read. King Mosiah taught his sons "in all the language of his fathers, that thereby they might become men of understanding; and that they might know concerning the prophecies which had been spoken by the mouths of their fathers, which were delivered them by the hand of the Lord" (Mosiah 1:2).

Mosiah wasn't just teaching his sons how to read so they could get ahead in the world; he was teaching them to read so they could immerse themselves in the scriptures and become spiritually wise.

The brass plates were preserved and taken to the promised land so that Lehi's family and his posterity would not forget who they were, "a chosen people," and would be reminded how they were to live as children of God. It is for the same purpose that the scriptures have been preserved for us in this day and at this time.

But gaining knowledge through scripture study requires some attributes and actions that most formal educational endeavors do not: sincere desire, unwavering faith, prayer, and the will and obedience to follow the Spirit's promptings. Virtually all humans upon earth, no matter what their mental capacity, can experience the joy and rewards of lifetime gospel study.

Scripture study does not require years of formal education to gain an understanding of essential gospel principles. This is illustrated by Peter and John in the book of Acts. The Jewish rulers were surprised. They assumed that gospel knowledge required some exhaustive, formal course of training. The scriptures tell us: "Now when they saw the boldness of Peter and John, and perceived that they were unlearned and ignorant men, they marvelled; and they took knowledge of them, that they had been with Jesus" (Acts 4:13).

Unlearned and ignorant in the eyes of the world, Peter and John had gained great gospel knowledge from listening and hearkening to the words of our Savior. The same can be true for each of us and for every member of our family. In gospel study, a master's degree in theology is far less valuable than the degree of knowledge we can all obtain from the Master Himself.

A critical component in gaining knowledge from the Savior is acting upon the principles He taught. In order to gain the greatest insights the scriptures have to offer, our study will focus not so much on places and names as on principles and doctrines. It is not simply book knowledge we are after but insights that will change the way we live and that will actually make a difference in our lives. We must see the scriptures for what they are: an instruction manual for becoming like our Savior.

Lifelong scripture study is an unending quest for spiritual insights and understanding and for the growth that results when we apply such insights in our lives. As Latter-day Saints, we understand that acquiring spiritual knowledge, having spiritual experiences, and developing our gifts and aptitudes are important to our mortal growth. In addition, we must develop our spiritual dispositions in relation to God, our Father, and His Son, Jesus Christ, and cultivate the qualities of faith and obedience that will invite the Holy Ghost into our lives. We also grow in spirit as we serve and care for our neighbors and the world around us. All of these elements of lifelong learning have eternal consequences, and their rewards are the essence of our mortal goal to obtain spiritual qualities and achievements. The results of our most important lifelong learning are not reflected in grades or degrees or honors but in who we become. Our aim is to develop eternal character values such as knowledge, hope, faith, charity, and love. This is the most important quest we have in learning.

Studying the scriptures helps us develop and progress as individuals. The scriptures are uniquely suited for lifelong study.

As we increase our spiritual, emotional, and mental capacity through the years, we qualify to gain new insights from the scriptures. How many times have you paused and pondered on a passage of scripture that you have read and passed over many times before and then, in a *revelatory* moment, have a *new awareness,* a *new understanding,* brought to your heart and mind granting additional insight—and that added insight solves a question, a problem, or one of life's challenges. That, my brothers and sisters, is the sweet mystery of lifelong learning—a sweet instant in a blessed moment in time when you experience a leap of faith and understanding.

It is for this reason that we have prayer before and after scripture study. The prayer before scripture study is to prepare us spiritually to receive the *revelatory moments* and a spiritual uplift. The prayer after scripture study is to give thanks and gratitude for that which has been given us.

The knowledge of the truths of the restored gospel of Jesus Christ is the most valuable knowledge we will ever possess. That knowledge is found in the word of God in the scriptures, through living prophets, and in the temple. The endowment is the eternal curriculum. In it we are taught where we came from and why we are here on earth, and we are even given the promise of achieving life eternal in the celestial kingdom if we obey the commandments and covenants we've taken upon ourselves.

Lifelong Learning—Past, Present, and Future

In addition to all the attributes we have talked about, lifelong learners see the connection between what we have learned in the past, what we are learning now, and what we can learn in the future. Lifelong learners are cumulative learners. They put together all that they have learned to help them. They will never dwell in the past because they are eager to explore the future. They will always be open to new concepts, being blessed with inquisitive minds that seek new knowledge on a daily basis.

Lifelong learners spend their lives doing better than their best! Sometimes our best is not good enough. Being challenged to do better than our best may seem unreasonable or defy intuitive logic, but personal progress is just simply that! The reality is that sometimes our best of today is not good enough to succeed in tomorrow's world.

For example, in the 2004 Olympics, American swimmer Michael Phelps, who we've heard a lot about lately, won the bronze medal in the men's 200-meter freestyle with a time of one minute forty-five seconds. Four years ago that was his best. But he knew that to win the gold medal in that event in 2008 he would have to do better than his best, so he set about training to meet that goal. Millions have had the opportunity to watch the Olympic saga that has unfolded as he did better than his previous best, setting a new world record of one minute forty-two seconds and winning a gold medal. In Beijing he shattered his own previous world record by a full second and improved upon Mark Spitz's winning time of 1972 by ten seconds. Think how fast that is! In fact, he shaved off over a full minute from the gold medal winning time in 1904 of two minutes forty-four seconds. Just imagine, today in just a minute they swim two laps of the pool! That's how far he would have finished ahead of the winner in 1904. It is remarkable that of Michael Phelps's 2008 gold medals, seven of his times beat world records; they were not only his own records but world records. The other, his eighth medal, set an Olympic record. Can you imagine being able to do that, and doing better than your best? What an example for us!

The reality is that if we do not improve our efforts and our achievements each day, our best in yesterday's past will not meet the demands of tomorrow's future. This principle of doing better than our best each day applies to both spiritual and temporal demands in our mortal lifetime of learning as we prepare, covenant, and meet the requirements of eternal salvation.

Sometimes the magnificent vista of learning is not limited by the capacity of our mind but rather by the artificial limitations we place upon ourselves and our ability to learn. We must expand the capacity of our mind. Just think of what our learning limitations were before the computer became a universal tool for research, learning, and Internet communication. It is hard for our grandchildren to imagine how we were educated without computers. (Or, for that matter, how we lived without a cell phone or survived without pizza as a diet staple. The list is endless.)

I would like to share with you a unique personal learning experience spanning over thirty years that relates to the emerging computer technology benefits in family history research. In the 1970s I observed Elder Theodore H. Burton presenting the future concept of computers being used for family records and research. He was even bold enough to teach and proclaim that the computer technology was given to man for use to hasten the day of family history, genealogy, and temple work.

Elder Burton's initial computer proclamation was met with understandable reservations: "Computers will always be too big and too expensive for personal use." "There will never be enough Church members with computers." "So few of the members are able to operate computers." "The detail and explanation required and the examination required to make personal research compatible with temple records are too complex." All seemed reasonable reservations for their time, but what of the future computer developments?

Today we are embarking on a new era of family history computer technology. With the upcoming release of the new system—already available in half of the temple districts around the world—we will be able to prepare and submit names of our ancestors for temple work from our homes using a new Internet-based system. This new system will help you readily see which ancestors need proxy temple ordinances and make it possible to print a summary page with a bar code that when scanned in the temple will print out a card for use in temple sessions. After an ordinance is completed, a record of the completed ordinance is typically available on this secure Web site within twenty-four hours.

Now, why do I tell this story to you as lifelong learners? I have a simple message. Never dwell on the past or attempt to protect your comfort zone against the inevitable changes required to meet the future advancements that will be needed. When Jesus said "It is finished" (John 19:30) as He died on the cross, it was the end of only one mission—the Atonement. He then went on to see those in eternity to shore them up and to give them hope (see D&C 138). We read in 3 Nephi that in yet another mission experience He also visited the faithful at the temple in the New World as a resurrected being, blessing them for their faithfulness. In our lives, as in the Savior's example, our endings only usher in new beginnings. The ending of one era ushers in a new era. Lifelong learners do not dwell on the past.

Past learning creates a valuable foundation of experience upon which to build, not a comfortable place to dwell for a lifetime.

Sometimes when we reach a milestone we viewed as an ultimate goal, we may find ourselves once the elation has passed almost depressed—for example, when you finish a mission or when the honeymoon is over. There is a moment of shocking, stark reality when you ask yourself, "What next? What do I do now?" At such times, remember the end is only the dawn of a new beginning.

As you stand atop any peak you have climbed, enjoy the moment of satisfaction in the present to look at the remarkable view and the progress you have made from the past. But then turn around to see what new peaks are now in sight and set a course to climb higher into the future. When you do this, the achievement of one goal set in the past will eventually pave the way to a higher goal of achievement in the future. As we contemplate the sacrifice and hard work that was required to achieve past goals, let us muster the confidence and determination needed to move on to greater heights.

Let me pause once again and talk to you from the depths of my heart about one of the unique experiences of learning. The real meaning of lifelong learning takes shape in the circle of past, present, and future—progressing as time moves on in its swift, inevitable pace. Time stops for no man. In fact, one of the few common possessions we all share is time. What we do with our time will determine the degree of lifelong learning and spiritual values we take to the eternities following our mortal test.

Also, let me spend a moment or two talking about a unique lifelong learning experience for a woman—*motherhood.*

Motherhood: The Ideal Opportunity for Lifelong Learning

Motherhood is the ideal opportunity for lifelong learning. A mother's learning grows as she nurtures the child in his or her development years. They are both learning and maturing together at a remarkable pace. It's exponential, not linear. Just think of the learning process of a mother throughout the lifetime of her children. Each child brings an added dimension to her learning because their needs are so varied and far-reaching.

For example, in the process of rearing her children, a mother studies such topics as child development; nutrition; health care; physiology; psychology; nursing with medical research and care; and educational tutoring in many diverse fields such as math, science, geography, literature, English, and foreign languages. She develops gifts such as music, athletics, dance, and public speaking. The learning examples could continue endlessly. Just think of the spiritual learning that is required as a mother teaches about gospel principles and prepares for teaching family home evening and auxiliary lessons in Primary, Relief Society, Young Women, and Sunday School.

My point is, my dear sisters—as well as for the brethren, who I hope are listening carefully—a mother's opportunity for lifelong learning and teaching is universal in nature. My dear sisters, don't ever sell yourself short as a woman or as a mother.

It never ceases to amaze me that the world would state that a woman is in a form of servitude that does not allow her to develop her gifts and talents. Nothing, absolutely nothing, could be further from the truth. Do not let the world define, denigrate, or limit your feelings of lifelong learning and the values of motherhood in the home—both here mortally and in the eternal learning and benefits you give to your children and to your companion.

Lifelong learning is essential to the vitality of the human mind, body, and soul. It enhances self-worth and self-actuation. Lifelong learning is invigorating mentally and is a great defense against aging, depression, and self-doubt. When we stand still in seeking new knowledge, our forward learning progress ceases and mental stagnation begins.

Progress and improvement are the essence of lifelong learning. You will not be surprised to know that there is only one ultimate goal: living a faithful life and enduring to the end worthy of eternal salvation and glory. All other goals and achievements are corollary to faithfully enduring to the end. Indeed, it is the plan of life set forth in the scriptures for our eternal benefit.

The learning process taught by Solomon in the Holy Bible in the book of Proverbs is helpful to aid us in understanding the nature of lifelong learning. "Happy is the man that findeth wisdom, and the man that getteth understanding" (Proverbs 3:13).

To further explain, we start with basic intelligence, or an IQ, which is God-given as one of the gifts bestowed on mankind. "The glory of God is intelligence, or, in other words, light and truth" (D&C 93:36).

To basic intelligence we add knowledge, which comes to us through learning and experience.

The sum of basic intelligence plus knowledge and experience equals wisdom. "Wisdom is the principal thing; therefore get wisdom: and with all thy getting get understanding" (Proverbs 4:7).

The world stops at wisdom's level of learning, but the scriptures teach "The Lord by *wisdom* hath founded the *earth*; by *understanding* hath he established the *heavens*" (Proverbs 3:19; emphasis added).

Wisdom plus the gifts of the Holy Ghost provide an understanding in our hearts. When we truly have an understanding and our hearts are softened, we will "no more desire to do evil" (Alma 19:33).

We will have "an eye single to the glory of God" (D&C 82:19) and desire to return with honor into the presence of our Heavenly Father and His Son, Jesus Christ.

Here is a lifetime homework assignment for you! Ponder and seek to acquire the remarkable attributes of a lifelong learner: courage, faithful desire, curiosity, humility, patience, and willingness to communicate. These are desirable character qualities. Ponder and ask yourself these questions: "What is the meaning and value of each of these qualities to me?" "How do these qualities apply to me?" "How am I going to have each of these qualities be part of my life?" Then for a few minutes ponder these qualities and ask yourself what you can do to enhance them in your character and in your life. Even if you only take one of the qualities and seek to improve yourself, it will make a difference. The reward will be great in your future for you and for those around you.

I hope you can see the value of reviewing your ultimate goals with an eye to lifelong learning perspectives and to life's cycle of past, present, and future. May your life be one of learning—growing in knowledge, intelligence, and wisdom while seeking spiritual values and characteristics that will bless you with the rewards of eternal life.

Seek to Know That God Lives

I give you my testimony that God lives and that we can learn not just to believe but to know that God lives. Seek that knowledge. It will be granted to you. Seek to know and to have those around you know, through your testimony, that Joseph Smith was a prophet of God and that in this last dispensation of the fulness of time we have had restored to us all that has ever been restored to mankind. Learn all that you can within our temples and our scriptures. Learn and conduct your life in such a way that you may return to the presence of our Father and His Son. I pray that our desires and goals will be to become lifelong learners to accomplish that end, in the name of Jesus Christ, amen.

Notes

1. Brigham Young, in *Journal of Discourses* (London: Latter-day Saints' Book Depot, 1854–86), 9:292.
2. Brigham Young, in *Journal of Discourses*, 12:124.
3. Ezra Taft Benson, "A New Witness for Christ," *Ensign*, November 1984, 6–7; quoting Joseph Smith, *History of the Church of Jesus Christ of Latter-day Saints*, ed. B. H. Roberts, 2nd ed. rev. (Salt Lake City: Deseret News, 1957), 4:461.

To Learn and to Teach More Effectively

Elder Richard G. Scott

Elder Richard G. Scott is a member of the Quorum of the Twelve Apostles.

This address was given at the Campus Education Week on August 21, 2007.

With you I sense the excitement and anticipation of inspiring events as we begin the eighty-fifth annual BYU Campus Education Week. I congratulate you for your decision to participate in this extraordinary activity that you may learn and develop from the experience shared here. There is nothing quite like it in scope and quality in all the world. I share with you a constant, continuing thirst to improve and grow through all of the various means of learning that the Lord has provided for us.

As I travel throughout the world, it is evident that knowledge is power. Some use it to their own personal advantage. Many of these employ knowledge improperly, severely limiting others in the use of their agency. Yet there are those whose learning, experience, and talent are used to lift, encourage, motivate, and bless others around them. I feel confident that you are among that group. Not only will you benefit from your invested time and effort here, but others will likewise be helped by how you apply and share what you learn. You are following the admonition of the Lord: "And as all have not faith, seek ye diligently and teach one another words of wisdom; yea, seek ye out of the best books words of wisdom; seek learning, even by study and also by faith" (D&C 88:118).

This year's theme, "The Dawning of a Brighter Day," is so appropriate. It emphasizes the wonder of the Restoration of the gospel in this dispensation. Any student of history is aware that the Restoration of the Church with its pure doctrine, priesthood authority, and divine guidance initiated an avalanche of discovery, enlightenment, and inventions that continue to powerfully lift mankind. How grateful I am to our Holy Father for the restoration of truth that came through the Prophet Joseph Smith to benefit all mankind. Joseph Smith is a motivating example of an individual who throughout his brief life continually sought knowledge and willingly shared it with others, even though it would cost him his life to do so.

My intent is to share thoughts of how to learn and how to teach effectively.

How to Learn More Effectively

There are a multitude of available paths through which we may learn and be perfected. Some of these include formal study, pondering, analysis, personal experience, careful observation, mentoring by others, observing outstanding role models, serving willingly, and learning from our own mistakes. It would be unrealistic to attempt to identify, even in headline form, the multitude of avenues through which knowledge flows and experience is gained. For that reason I have chosen to speak of what for me is the most effective path to truth and to the inexhaustible source of guidance and inspiration from our Heavenly Father and His Beloved Son. That path is by spiritual guidance through the prompting of the Holy Ghost. Together we will lay a foundation to understand spiritual guidance and to discuss how to obtain it and how to share it. My sincere desire is to provide motivation for you to expand your capacity to gain knowledge, for your eternal benefit and the blessing of those with whom you will share it.

Also, there will be mentioned some of the important truths I have learned from seeking the guidance of the Holy Spirit. And since I recognize that many of you are motivated to be here by the desire to help others learn and live truth, I will suggest ways that you might teach these truths. It would be much easier for me to do this if we could have two-way communication. Fortunately, you will almost always have the privilege of encouraging interaction with those you teach, even if it is one-on-one with a family member. Your instructions will be more beneficial and enduring when you promote that participation.

As we begin I will share a gospel truth that, if communicated effectively and used consistently in your life, would entirely justify every effort you have made to be at Education Week, if that is the only thing you do here. It will help you obtain the most benefit from this hour together, from the balance of your participation here, and in other significant events throughout your life. I notice that many of you have come prepared to take notes on what you hear. While that is of great benefit, I will share a pattern that will provide you even greater access to truth. It is summarized in this statement of principle:

Throughout the remainder of my life, I will seek to learn by what I hear, see, and feel. I will write down the important things I learn, and I will do them.

I suggest that you write this down. If I were to end this message at this point, you would have received one of the most meaningful ways to learn that I could impart. If the principle just shared doesn't seem that important, think again. Many of the vital lessons I have learned and treasured, I have learned by carefully following it.

How to Respond to Spiritual Promptings

You can learn vitally important things by what you *hear* and *see* and, even more, by what you *feel*, as prompted by the Holy Ghost. Many individuals limit their learning primarily to what they *hear* or *read*. Be wise. Develop the skill of also learning by what you *see* and particularly by what the Holy Ghost prompts you to *feel*. Consciously and consistently seek to learn by what you *feel*. Your capacity to do so will expand through repeated practice. Significant faith and effort are required to learn by what you feel from the Spirit. Ask in faith for such help. Live to be worthy of such guidance.

Write down in a secure place the important things you learn from the Spirit. You will find that as you record a precious impression, often others will come that you would not have otherwise received. Also, the spiritual knowledge you gain will be available throughout your life. Always, day or night, wherever you are, whatever you are doing, seek to recognize and respond to the direction of the Spirit. Have available a piece of paper or a card to record such guidance.

Express gratitude to the Lord for the spiritual guidance you receive and obey it. This practice will reinforce your capacity to learn by the Spirit. It will enhance the guidance of the Lord in your life. You will learn more as you act upon the knowledge, experience, and inspiration communicated to you by the Holy Ghost.

Spiritual guidance is direction, enlightenment, knowledge, and motivation you receive from Jesus Christ through the Holy Spirit. It is personalized instruction adapted to your individual needs by One who understands them perfectly. Spiritual guidance is a gift of incomparable worth bestowed upon those who seek it, live worthy of it, and express gratitude for it.

The scriptures define how to qualify for spiritual guidance. Elder Bruce R. McConkie wisely counseled, "However talented men may be in administrative matters; however eloquent they may be in expressing their views; however learned they may be in the worldly things, they will be denied the sweet whisperings of the Spirit that might have been theirs unless they pay the price of studying, pondering, and praying about the scriptures."[1]

Over time, through prayer and pondering applicable scriptures, I have found the following pattern for gaining spiritual direction helpful.

To acquire spiritual guidance and to obey it with wisdom, one must:
- Seek divine light in humility
- Exercise faith, especially in Jesus Christ
- Strive diligently to keep His commandments
- Repent constantly
- Pray continually
- Hearken to spiritual guidance
- Express gratitude for guidance received

May that suggestion be of some benefit in your quest for spiritual guidance.

Teaching Others to Learn from the Spirit

Now we will review how others could be taught the principle of learning I mentioned earlier that you can use. First, I would encourage each one taught to write down the principle: *Throughout the remainder of my life, I will seek to learn by what I hear, see, and feel. I will write down the important things I learn, and I will do them.*

Then I would explain how to use each of the three avenues of communication, to hear, to see, and to feel. Further I would seek to commit each one to live that principle, for every student who would consistently do that would be blessed with greater inspired direction in his or her life.

I would then illustrate with the following series of graphics how to enhance learning.

1. My intent is to show some ways you can help others to qualify to be led by the Spirit and to realize that when that direction comes, it should be recorded and obeyed.

2. Those you teach live in a world subject to challenges and temptations. I am convinced that without the help of the Spirit an individual will have difficulty avoiding transgression in the world today. Should the wrong choices be made, that person becomes bound by sin.

3. You can encourage a student to live so as to be influenced by the Spirit and to recognize its guidance in order to be blessed by obedience to its direction. You can play a vital role in that process.

As you teach the appropriate doctrine and help explain how the Lord communicates through the Spirit, your students will *experience* being led by the Spirit. They will learn the principles upon which such communication is based. As they apply those principles, they will make the correct choices in life.

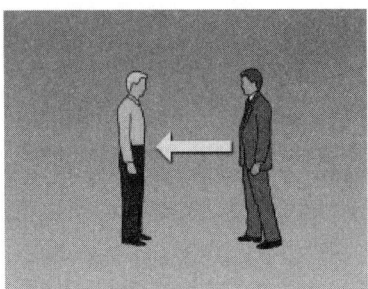

4. All too often a teacher's relation to a student is one of giving counsel with little or no interaction. Often there is no explanation of the reasons why there are commandments, rules, and standards. The teacher becomes just a talking head.

Most of the teaching in the world is based on one of the five senses—hear, see, touch, smell, or taste. In your classroom, you can teach by the power of the Spirit.

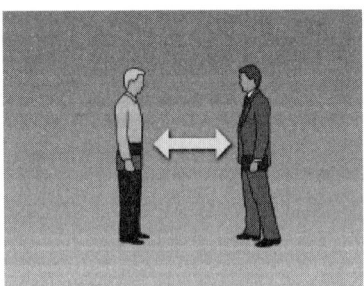

5. Such communication begins by your encouraging each one you teach to participate rather than be a passive listener. In this way you can assess their understanding of what is taught, create a feeling of ownership, and also learn from them. More important, their decision to participate is an exercise in agency that permits the Holy Ghost to communicate a personalized message suited to their individual needs. Creating an atmosphere of participation en-

hances the probability that the Spirit will teach more important lessons than you can communicate.

6. That participation will bring into their lives the direction of the Spirit. When you encourage students to raise their hands to respond to a question, while they may not realize it, they signify to the Holy Ghost their willingness to learn. That use of moral agency will allow that Spirit to motivate and give them more powerful guidance during your time together. Participation allows individuals to *experience* being led by the Spirit. They learn to recognize and feel what spiritual guidance is. It is through the repeated process of feeling impressions, recording them, and obeying them that one learns to depend on the direction of the Spirit more than on communication through the other five senses.

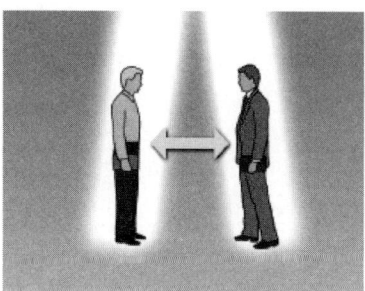

7. Your capacity to teach is enhanced by the direction you receive from the Holy Spirit. Simply stated, truth presented in an environment of true love and trust qualifies an individual for the confirming witness of the Holy Spirit.

8. If you accomplish nothing else in your relationship with your students than to help them recognize and follow the promptings of the Spirit, you will bless their lives immeasurably and eternally. To do this you must constantly seek the guidance of the Spirit to know what to say and how to say it.

I am convinced that there is no simple formula or technique that I could give you or that you could give your students that would immediately facilitate mastering the ability to be guided by the Holy Spirit. Nor do I believe that the Lord will ever allow someone to conceive a pattern that would invariably and immediately open the channels of spiritual communication. We grow when we labor to recognize the guidance of the Holy Ghost as we struggle to communicate our needs to our Father in Heaven in moments of dire need or overflowing gratitude. Each time we do that we are taking another step in fulfilling the purpose of our being here on earth.

Our Father expects us to learn how to obtain that divine help by exercising faith in Him and in His Holy Son. Were we to receive inspired guidance just for the asking, we would become weak and ever more dependent on Him. He knows that essential personal growth will come as we struggle to learn how to be led by the Spirit. That struggle develops our immortal character as we perfect our capacity to identify His will through the whisperings of the Holy Ghost. What may appear initially to be a daunting task will become much easier over time as we consistently strive to recognize the feelings awakened by the Spirit. Our confidence in the direction we receive through the Holy Ghost will also become stronger.

Easy things never produce much beneficial fruit. Neither our Father in Heaven nor His Holy Son take delight in seeing you struggle to overcome obstacles, resolve questions, or find solutions to complex and challenging problems. However, they do rejoice when you willingly recognize that these steps are steps to growth which lead to action that molds your character.

Treasuring Up Sacred Impressions

Have you learned the enduring value of keeping a journal of the very important spiritual experiences or sacred impressions that the Lord has communicated to you? I do not keep a detailed journal of all the events each day, but I try to keep record of some very important matters. The spiritual ones are in a sacred password-protected journal that no one else can access. When I feel authorized by the Holy Ghost, I take some of the truths learned and put them in my family journal or share them in a public message. This is consistent with a principle that the scriptures confirm is true. Some personal matters are for our guidance and edification to help us grow and improve our character, our devotion, and our testimony. These things are not intended for other individuals. Much like a patriarchal blessing is tailored for the person to whom it is given, such matters should be kept reverently protected because of their inherent sacred nature. Any sacred matter that the Lord wants others to know, He can communicate to them directly through the Spirit if they are worthy and in tune.

To confirm that what I have been talking about is not just pure theory, I will now mention some of the priceless truths I have learned through spiritual guidance over many years.

The scriptures teach and I have been led to confirm that we will never be prompted by the Holy Ghost to do something we cannot do. It may require extraordinary effort and much time, patience, prayer, and obedience, but we can do it.

Repeatedly I have been impressed to learn that to reach a goal never before attained one must do things never before done.

I have been taught that we can make many choices in life, but we cannot determine our final destiny. Our actions do that. It can appear that we control outcomes in our life, but we do not. Worthiness, righteousness, faith in Jesus Christ, and the plan of our Father assure a pleasant productive future, while lying, cheating, or violating the laws of personal purity assure a life of misery here on earth and beyond the veil, unless there is the requisite repentance.

It is important not to judge ourselves by what we think we know of our own potential. We should trust the Lord and what He can do with our dedicated heart and willing mind (see D&C 64:34).

I have been taught by the Holy Spirit and the observation of others that concepts like faith, prayer, love, and humility hold no great significance and produce no miracles until they become a living part of the individual through his or her own experience, aided by the sweet promptings of the Spirit.

We all will have adversity; it is a part of life. We will all have it because we need it for growth and the forging of our righteous character. I have learned that the Lord has a consummate capacity to judge our intent. He is concerned about what we are becoming by the choices we make. He has an individual plan for each of us. This concept is very comforting when we consider how to understand difficult matters such as the early death of someone who seems to be so needed on earth. It is most helpful when we struggle with illness or a severe handicap or try to assess another's tragic suicide.

I have been led through personal experience to understand an important truth. I know Satan has absolutely no power to force a determined righteous individual because the Lord protects that person from him. Satan can tempt; he can threaten; he can attempt to appear to have such power; but he does not possess it.

I have learned that our mind can strengthen an impression of the Holy Ghost or sadly, can totally destroy it by casting it out as something unimportant or the product of our own imagination. When spiritual guidance comes, it is well to remember this comment of the Prophet Joseph Smith, "God judges men according to the use they make of the light which He gives them."[2]

When facing adversity we can be led to ask many questions. Some of them serve a useful purpose; others do not. It really does no good to ask questions that reflect opposition to the will of God. Willing sacrifice of deeply held personal desires in favor of God's will is generally very hard to do. Yet when done, we are in the strongest position to receive the maximum help from our loving Heavenly Father. Accepting His will, even when it is not fully understood, brings great peace and, over time, understanding.

It is sometimes very hard to discern an answer to prayer for a matter for which we have very deep personal feelings or something which causes strong emotions to arise within us. That is why it is important to receive valid, inspired counsel when one finds himself or herself in such a circumstance.

In a quiet moment of pondering I learned that there is a relationship between faith and character. The greater our faith in Jesus Christ, the stronger our character and increased character enhances our ability to exercise even greater faith.

The Spirit has taught that Satan doesn't have to tempt us to do bad things. He can accomplish much of his objective by distracting us with many acceptable things, thus keeping us from accomplishing the essential ones. We need to frustrate that distraction by identifying what is critically important in our lives. We must give the cream of our effort to accomplish those things. Where there is limited time or resources, this pattern may require that some good activities be set aside.

On occasion the Lord will give us vital spiritual guidance by inspiring others to share what they have learned. Such mentors can greatly enrich our life through thoughtful communication of their knowledge and experience. We also can identify living or deceased mentors by careful study and emulation of their productive lives. I am confident that the recent passing of President James E. Faust has brought to the mind of thousands of individuals he has touched personally gratitude for his encouragement and motivation. He had the exceptional capacity to lift and build other individuals. He chose valid reasons to congratulate others as he spoke of them with sincerity and integrity. The result was to edify, lift, and help them to explore a course of life that would bring each greater success and happiness. His encouragement was often brief and concise, yet most effective and enduring.

One of the most memorable and powerful patterns of communication by the Spirit is through dreams. I have learned that when the transition from being fully asleep to being fully awake is almost imperceptible, it is a signal that the Lord has taught something very important through a dream. When this occurs, I recognize the need to ponder what I remember of the dream to seek to understand it and its application in my life. Sometimes the dream is symbolic and prayer is required so that through the Holy Ghost the Lord can interpret or clarify the lessons to be understood and applied.

Throughout the majority of my teenage and adult life, I have greatly appreciated *mercy*. It was through a vivid dream that I learned also to cherish *justice*. Justice provides order and control in our Father's plan of happiness. It assures that whatever we have earned through worthy effort will ever be ours, such as knowledge, the love of dear ones, and the eternal benefits of ordinances, including those of the temple. Justice assures that no power can take these precious things from us. We could lose them through disobedience, but who would want to do that?

The Savior's injunction to "ask, and ye shall receive; knock, and it shall be opened unto you" (3 Nephi 27:29) is a gate to spiritual guidance. I have been taught that gentle promptings will encourage us to make the right decisions. When carefully observed, these gentle impressions to our heart can be followed by specific counsel given to our mind. That counsel leads us to know what to do with greater precision. Such detailed direction comes when we readily respond to the initial promptings of the Spirit. At times such spiritual guidance can indicate or imply events that will occur later in life. Our acceptance of such prompting and willingness to obey it does not mean that the will of the Lord will be changed. It does mean that the impact on our life will be different. There will be far more significant consequence because of our willingness to obey the counsel given by such sacred guidance of the Holy Spirit.

There is one last priceless gem of spiritual guidance I would share. It has taken a very long time to recognize. Forced obedience yields no enduring fruit. That is why both our Father in Heaven and the Savior are willing to entreat, to prompt, to encourage, and to patiently wait for us to recognize precious spiritual guidance from Them. Once it took me over ten years to discover the answer to an extremely important matter for which I had prayed consistently and earnestly. The complete answer came as I was able to assemble portions of the solution communicated to me in differing ways and at differing times. I was not given the answer directly, but I was patiently and lovingly led to find it.

I close with my testimony. I will try to follow the excellent counsel given by President Spencer W. Kimball. He taught: "A testimony is not an exhortation; a testimony is not a sermon; . . . it is not a travelogue. . . . Just tell how you feel inside. That is the testimony. The moment you begin preaching to others, your testimony ended. Just tell us how you feel, what your mind and heart and every fiber of your body tells you."[3]

I know that the things I have shared are true for I have learned them. They have been confirmed by the gentle promptings of the Holy Ghost. May some of them be of benefit to you. I positively know that Jesus Christ lives and as one of His Apostles bear solemn witness that He is a glorified, resurrected, personage of perfect love. He guides His Church on earth. He loves you. During your presence here He will prompt you. As you seek that prompting to identify it, He will guide your life. He is our Master, our Redeemer, our Savior. I love Him. With every capacity that I possess I bear witness that He lives. In the name of Jesus Christ, amen.

Notes

1. Bruce R. McConkie, regional representatives seminar, April 2, 1982.
2. Joseph Smith, *Teachings of the Prophet Joseph Smith*, comp. Joseph Fielding Smith (Salt Lake City: Deseret Book, 1976), 303.
3. *Teachings of Presidents of the Church: Spencer W. Kimball* (Salt Lake City: The Church of Jesus Christ of Latter-day Saints, 2006), 76–77.

King Benjamin delivered one of the most masterful discourses ever given on the Atonement.

© Intellectual Reserve, Inc.

Teaching the Atonement

Elder Tad R. Callister

Elder Tad R. Callister *is a member of the Second Quorum of the Seventy.*

How can we as teachers of the restored gospel effectively teach the sublime and deep doctrine of the Atonement? How have the prophets done so? And what can we learn from them?[1]

Although prophets through the ages have reflected varying talents and unique teaching skills, certain underlying principles occur again and again in their teaching ministries. Set forth below are some teaching techniques and resources used by the prophets to explain the atoning doctrine and its infinite implications.

A Spiritual Shot across the Bow

King Benjamin called his subjects together—but not for a day of entertainment. If any had come with spiritual thimbles to receive his words, he was quick to inform them of the need for much larger receptacles: "I have not commanded you to come up hither to *trifle* with the words which I shall speak, but that you should hearken unto me, and open your ears that ye may hear, and your hearts that ye may understand, and your minds that the mysteries of God may be unfolded to your view" (Mosiah 2:9; emphasis added). His introduction was a warning shot that ears needed to be spiritually attuned and hearts softened to receive the message of supernal import that was about to follow. He then gave one of the most masterful sermons ever delivered on the Atonement. Years later, Elder Bruce R. McConkie began his never-to-be-forgotten sermon on the atoning sacrifice with these profound words: "I feel, and the Spirit seems to accord, that the most important doctrine I can declare, and the most powerful testimony I can bear, is of the atoning sacrifice of the Lord Jesus Christ."[2]

Just like King Benjamin, he first set the stage before launching into his inspired message. As a result, ears perked up, minds became more focused, and hearts yielded to receive the spiritual reservoir that was about to be released. The impact of these messages was life-changing for many. Those who heard the words of King Benjamin cried with one accord, "We believe all the words thou hast spoken unto us; and . . . we have no more disposition to do evil, but to do good continually" (Mosiah 5:2).

These prophets began their sermons by firing a spiritual shot across the bow. It was a warning, a wake-up call, that the message to follow deserved far more than the listener's casual attention. It required an intense alertness of all his spiritual faculties. Why? Because these prophets knew that the beautiful but difficult doctrine of the Atonement can be comprehended only by the spiritually prepared. Their messages are poignant reminders of the spiritual tone we ought to set *before* we commence teaching what Robert L. Millet calls "the doctrine of doctrines."[3]

Laying the Groundwork

A person could never master calculus without first mastering algebra. A certain order of events is required in the learning process. Isaiah taught, "Whom shall he teach knowledge? and whom shall he make to understand doctrine?" Then, he gave the simple but profound formula for mastering the doctrines of the Church: "precept upon precept; line upon line" (Isaiah 28:9–10). President Ezra Taft Benson taught, "No one adequately and properly knows why he needs Christ until he understands and accepts the doctrine of the Fall and its effect upon all mankind."[4]

Students quickly learn the impossibility of adequately comprehending the Atonement without first understanding the Fall. Lehi gave a magnificent discourse on the Atonement (see 2 Nephi 2). In the course of it, he first explained the conditions that existed in the Garden of Eden.

Then, he followed his introduction with a succinct summary of why the Savior came: "The Messiah cometh in the fulness of time, that he may redeem the children of men from the fall" (2 Nephi 2:26). Thus, we learn that the Atonement was necessary to correct certain conditions brought about by the

Fall (that is, physical and spiritual death). Alma, in counseling his wayward son Corianton, discerned, "I perceive there is somewhat more which doth worry your mind, which ye cannot understand—which is concerning the justice of God in the punishment of the sinner." Then, he said, "Now behold, my son, I will explain this thing unto thee" (Alma 42:1–2). In the next eleven verses, Alma laid the groundwork for his answer by detailing the conditions in the Garden of Eden and the consequences of the Fall. Only then did he proceed to explain the relationships among justice, mercy, and the Atonement.

Because of the need to understand the Fall before we can fully comprehend the purposes of the Atonement, I have found the following chart useful in helping students grasp how the Atonement corrects or redeems the "negative" consequences of the Fall:

Before the Fall	**After the Fall**	**After the Atonement**
1. Immortality (+) Genesis 2:17	1. Mortality (-) Genesis 2:17	1. Resurrection (+) (unconditional for all) 1 Corinthians 15:20–22
2. Lived in God's presence (+) Genesis 3:8; Moses 4:14	2. Spiritual death (-) a. First spiritual death (born outside God's presence) D&C 29:41; 2 Nephi 9:6 b. Second spiritual death (separated from God because of individual sin) Alma 34:15–16; Alma 42:13–16	2. Overcame spiritual death (+) a. Unconditional because everyone returns to God's presence for judgment purposes 2 Nephi 2:20; 2 Nephi 9:38; Alma 12:15; Alma 42:23; Helaman 14:15–18; Mormon 9:12–14 b. Conditional because second spiritual death is overcome only if we repent Helaman 14:15–18; Moroni 9:12–14
3. Innocent (-) 2 Nephi 2:23	3. Knowledge of good and evil (+) Genesis 3:5; Alma 42:3	3. Unlimited knowledge of good and evil (+) John 14:26
4. Childless (-) 2 Nephi 2:23	4. Children (+) 2 Nephi 2:25; Moses 5:11	4. Children forever (+) D&C 132:19

The Book of Mormon Comes to the Rescue

The doctrines of the Fall and the Atonement are the centerpiece of Christianity, yet many misconceptions exist concerning their underlying principles because the Bible, as inspired as it is, has had "many plain and precious things taken away" (1 Nephi 13:28) from its original manuscripts. As a result, "an exceedingly great many do stumble, yea, insomuch that Satan hath great power over them" (1 Nephi 13:29). Elder McConkie once offered this challenge: "Choose the one hundred most basic doctrines of the gospel, and under each doctrine make two parallel columns, one headed *Bible* and the other *Book of Mormon*. Then place in these columns what each book of scripture says about each doctrine. The end result will show, without question, that in ninety-five of the one hundred cases, the Book of Mormon teaching is clearer, plainer, more expansive, and better than the biblical word. If there is any question in anyone's mind about this, let him take the test—a personal test."[5]

Nowhere is this invitation more applicable than with respect to the Atonement. Without the Book of Mormon, many misconceptions have arisen in the Christian world on this keystone doctrine. For example:

First misconception: Many teach that Adam and Eve would have had children in the Garden of Eden if they had been allowed to remain. After their transgression in the garden, the Lord said that "in sorrow thou shalt bring forth children" (Genesis 3:16). Accordingly, some have interpreted this to mean that if no transgression had occurred, Adam and Eve would have had children without sorrow in the Garden of Eden. But the Book of Mormon reveals the truth: "And they would have had no children" (2 Nephi 2:23; see also Moses 5:11).

Second misconception: Some teach that Adam and Eve were living in a state of bliss—of unparalleled joy—in the garden. Again, the Book of Mormon teaches the truth: "They would have remained in a state of innocence, having no joy, for they knew no misery" (2 Nephi 2:23). As a result of the first two misconceptions, much of the Christian world believes the Fall was a tragic step backward. They have innocently, but incorrectly, concluded that if Adam had not fallen, all of us would have been born in the Garden of Eden and thereafter lived in a state of eternal bliss. Such reasoning, however, would have negated the need for the Atonement, an event that was foreordained in the premortal life (see Ether 3:14). John so witnessed when he spoke of the Savior as "the Lamb slain from the foundation of the world" (Revelation 13:8).

Third misconception: There are those who teach that because of the Fall, all infants are tainted with original sin. Mormon gave a scathing rebuke to those who so believed: "I know that it is solemn mockery before God, that ye should baptize little children." He quoted the Savior in explaining the reason why: "The curse of Adam is taken from them in me, that it hath no power over them" (Moroni 8:8, 9).

Fourth misconception: Some people believe that grace alone can save us, regardless of any works on our part. Nephi puts the doctrines of faith and works in their proper perspective: "For we know that it is by grace that we are saved, *after* all we can do" (2 Nephi 25:23; emphasis added). We do not earn our salvation, but Nephi taught we must contribute the best we have to offer. C. S. Lewis hit the nail on the head while discussing the age-old debate between faith and works: "It does seem to me like asking which blade in a pair of scissors is most necessary."[6]

Fifth misconception: Another fallacy is that the physical Resurrection of the Savior is merely symbolic and that we will be resurrected without the "limitations" of a physical body. Alma, however, left no doubt about the corporeal nature of the Resurrection: "The soul shall be restored to the body, and the body to the soul . . . yea, even a hair of the head shall not be lost" (Alma 40:23).

Sixth misconception: Many people teach that the Atonement does not have the power to transform us into gods; in fact, according to them, such a thought is blasphemous. The Savior Himself, however, extended the divine challenge: "What manner of men ought ye to be? Verily I say unto you, even as I am" (3 Nephi 27:27). The concluding chapter in the Book of Mormon then reinforces this lofty doctrine: "Yea, come unto Christ, and be perfected in him by the grace of God, through the shedding of the blood of Christ" (Moroni 10:32–33).

Although Nephi knew that many plain and precious truths would be deleted from the Bible, he likewise knew that the Book of Mormon, among other sacred writings, would come to the rescue: "These last records, which thou hast seen among the Gentiles, shall establish the truth of the first, which are of the twelve apostles of the Lamb, and shall make known the plain and precious things which have been taken away from them" (1 Nephi 13:40).

President Ezra Taft Benson spoke of the absolute need for the Book of Mormon to comprehend the divinity and Atonement of the Savior: "Much of the Christian world today rejects the divinity of the Savior. They question His miraculous birth, His perfect life, and the reality of His glorious resurrection. The Book of Mormon teaches in plain and unmistakable terms about the truth of all of those. It also provides the most complete explanation of the doctrine of the Atonement. Truly, this divinely inspired book is a keystone in bearing witness to the world that Jesus is the Christ."[7]

The Book of Mormon is a gold mine for discovering the magnificent truths of the Atonement. The following are but a sample of the many chapters filled with golden nuggets for those who are willing to do some panning:

2 Nephi 2 (Lehi)	Alma 40 and 42 (Alma)
2 Nephi 9 (Jacob)	Helaman 14 (Samuel)
Mosiah 2–5 (King Benjamin)	3 Nephi 11 (the Savior)
Alma 34 (Amulek)	Moroni 10 (Moroni)

As we feast upon the words of the Book of Mormon, we will connect the spiritual dots that unveil the glorious picture of the Savior's atoning sacrifice.

The Power of a Good Question

How is the Savior's Atonement infinite? Did the Savior suffer for sins both in the Garden of Gethsemane and on the cross? Could He, a perfect man, understand what it is like to have weaknesses—to be rejected? Was there a backup plan if He chose not to proceed? Could a person suffer for his or her own sins and be redeemed?

The power of a good question is of inestimable worth. In many ways, it is like a mental alarm clock that awakens us out of our mental doldrums. It is a catalyst that jump-starts our mental engines. It causes the cerebral wheels to move, and thrusts upon us a certain uneasiness, an anxiety that triggers a fixation on the subject at hand until relief comes only in the form of an answer that is both satisfying to the mind and acceptable to the heart. Until that answer comes, it is like staring at a crooked picture without being able to fix it or working on a puzzle with one piece missing—there is an irresistible urge to straighten the painting and a compelling urge to find and place the final piece of the puzzle in its rightful place. Until that happens, one's mind is in overdrive—considering all the options, weighing, sifting, and sorting until the answer comes. A tremendous difference exists between being told the answer and discovering it. It is somewhat like being given a picture versus painting one, receiving a book compared to writing one, or listening to Rachmaninoff's Piano Concerto No. 3 versus playing it. Discovering the answer brings immense satisfaction, gives ownership, and makes a permanent deposit in our memory bank—not just some "in-and-out" entry.

There are many types of questions. There are factual questions to acquire background information. Such inquiries, however, are usually a means, not an end. For example: Where was the Savior born? How long was He in the Garden of Gethsemane? These questions are helpful in setting the stage, but in and of themselves, they do little to stir human emotions or fire human resolve. Nonetheless, a factual setting is often a necessary prerequisite to discovering the greater truths.

There are questions that elicit a self-evaluation. God's question to Adam, "Where art thou?" (Genesis 3:9) was more than a request for Adam's physical location. It was also an inquiry into Adam's spiritual standing. The climax of Alma's sermon to the people of Zarahemla consisted of eleven consecutive, introspective questions, such as, "Have ye spiritually been born of God? Have ye received his image in your countenances? Have ye experienced this mighty change in your hearts?" (Alma 5:14). A thoughtful teacher might ask similar questions that require self-evaluation of one's faith and worthiness: Do you believe you can be totally cleansed of your sins because of the Savior's infinite sacrifice? Do you have faith that His Atonement provides a remedy for each of your weaknesses, sins, infirmities, and shortcomings? Do you have a broken heart and a contrite spirit?

There are other questions that heighten our level of commitment. Three times the Savior asked Peter, "Lovest thou me?" (John 21:15–17). No doubt, Peter responded each time with greater passion—an even deeper commitment to the Holy One. Teachers might ask similar questions: Do we love the Savior enough to forgive others as He forgives us? Do we appreciate His sacrifice to the extent we are willing to consecrate our all in furthering His cause?"

Questions can also be effective answers. Corianton wondered why the coming of Christ "should be known so long beforehand." The answer his father Alma gave was in the form of a series of questions: "Behold, I say unto you, is not a soul at this time as precious unto God as a soul will be at the time of his coming? Is it not as necessary that the plan of redemption should be made known unto this people as well as unto their children?" (Alma 39:17–18). Suppose a student were to ask, "Is the Atonement retroactive? Could the people of Old Testament times receive its benefits *before* the purchase price was paid?" Resisting the temptation to give the instant answer, a wise teacher might respond with another question, "Do we have anything in our current society that allows us to enjoy the benefits *before* we pay the price?" The resulting discussion might reflect the credit card as an example. This outcome might further lead to the fact that the Savior's credit was pure "gold" in the premortal existence because He always kept His word. Accordingly, under the laws of justice, the benefits of His Atonement could be enjoyed before the purchase price was paid because there was no doubt He would pay "the bill" when it was presented to Him in the garden and on the cross (see Alma 39 headnote and Mosiah 3:13).

A good question can often be the springboard for an entire sermon or class discussion. So it was for Amulek, who discerned "that the great question which is in your minds is whether the word be in the Son of God, or whether there shall be no Christ" (Alma 34:5). In response, Amulek delivered his wonderful sermon on the infinite nature of the Atonement.

And Then More

How does a mere mortal understand and grasp the Savior's love and sacrifice of infinite proportions? Of course a mortal cannot fully do so. But the prophets have done their best to help bridge the gap by comparing the Atonement to two of the most passionate, loving relationships known by man and then suggesting that it is all this plus more, much more.

One example addresses the story of Abraham and Isaac. In speaking of Abraham's sacrifice of Isaac, Jacob notes that the event was "a *similitude* of God and his Only Begotten Son" (Jacob 4:5; emphasis added). It would be difficult, if not impossible, for a father to contemplate a greater trial than to sacrifice his beloved son, the very one through whom the blessings of eternity were to flow. What father cannot empathize with Abraham as he bound his son and then stretched forth the knife to spill the lifeblood of this promised child? The pain must have been bitterly acute—the emotions heart wrenching—as he raised his hand to make the fatal plunge. But at such a moment, the angel of mercy released him: "Lay not thine hand upon the lad, neither do thou any thing unto him: for now I know that thou fearest God, seeing thou has not withheld thy son, thine only son from me" (Genesis 22:12). Abraham then found a ram caught in the thicket to be the "sacrificial lamb" in place of his son; but for our Father in Heaven, there was no ram to be caught in the thicket, no angel of mercy to stay the hand of death. Our Father's sacrifice would be all that Abraham encountered, *and then more.*

Isaiah knew there was no love like the love of a mother for her nursing child. And so he asked, "Can a woman forget her sucking child?" As unlikely as that possibility might be, he used it as his spiritual yardstick to show that God's infinite love encompasses a mother's love—*and then more:* "Yea, they may forget, yet, will I not forget thee. Behold, I have graven thee upon the palms of my hands" (Isaiah 49:15–16). Lest there be any question, the nail marks of the cross would be a tangible reminder that His love transcended even the love of a mother for her infant child.

These examples cause us to plumb the depths of our emotional reservoirs. They are windows to the infinite. Although we cannot fully comprehend, they nonetheless help us momentarily glimpse the unbounded love of the Father and the Son.

The Pure Doctrine of the Atonement

Perhaps the most masterful discourse on the Atonement in the revealed scriptures is that delivered by King Benjamin (see Mosiah 2–5). In his own words, he said, "I have spoken plainly unto you that ye might understand" (2:40). With clarity and conciseness, he proceeded line by line and verse by verse with compelling logic and an uncompromising testimony that cannot be refuted by the mind or spirit. This sermon is a spiritual missile launched with laser precision to the center of the soul. It is as though the spiritually attuned are receiving the wondrous atoning truths in undiluted fashion, akin to a spiritual transfusion of pure doctrine. There is no need for outside collaborating sources or historical evidences. None of that is necessary because these spiritually mature Saints are ready and eager to receive the atoning doctrine in its fullest dose. And so they do.

Set forth below is the doctrine of the Atonement in the most concise and accurate way I can express it. Perhaps when we are spiritually prepared and our students are spiritually ready, we can, like King Benjamin, give the full dose and "tell it like it is" so that "he that preacheth and he that receiveth, understand one another, and both are edified and rejoice together" (D&C 50:22).

The doctrine of the Atonement is the most supernal, mind-expanding, passionate doctrine this world or universe will ever know. It is this doctrine that gives life and breath and substance to every gospel principle and ordinance. It is the spiritual reservoir that feeds the streams of faith, provides the cleansing powers to the waters of baptism, and supplies the healing balm to the wounded soul. It is the focal point of the sacrament, temple, and other gospel ordinances. It is the rock foundation upon which all hope in this life and eternity is predicated.

By definition, the Atonement is the foreordained mission of the Savior. It is that love displayed, that power manifested, and that suffering endured by Jesus Christ in three principal locations—namely, the Garden of Gethsemane, the cross of Calvary, and the tomb of Arimathea. It is the universal act of supreme submission in which the Savior completely yielded His will to that of the Father.

The Atonement was necessitated by the Fall of Adam. Lehi wrote, "The Messiah cometh in the fulness of time, that he may redeem the children of men from the fall" (2 Nephi 2:26). Adam's transgression was called the Fall because Adam and Eve fell from the presence of God and, in addition, fell from immortality to mortality. Thus, one of the prime purposes of the Atonement was to redeem men and women from the negative consequences of the Fall. The Savior did this in part by dying on the cross and subsequently bringing about the Resurrection for everyone. Paul so testified: "As in Adam all die, even so in Christ shall all be made alive" (1 Corinthians 15:22). In addition, the Savior suffered for everyone's sins, as evidenced by His bleeding from every pore, which act brought about the condition of repentance. Through His stripes, we can be healed. So complete is this healing process that Isaiah taught, "Though your sins be as scarlet, they shall be white as snow" (Isaiah 1:18).

But there is yet another purpose of the Atonement—it is not just to redeem us (that is, to reconcile the Fall) but to perfect us. The Atonement was designed to do more than return us to the starting line, more than just wipe the slate clean, more than make us innocent. It was designed to provide us with heavenly endowments that would help us achieve godlike perfection. How is that accomplished? Because of the Atonement, we are cleansed in the waters of baptism. Because of that cleansing, we are eligible to receive the gift of the Holy Ghost; and with that gift, we are entitled to the gifts of the Spirit (that is, knowledge, patience, love, and so forth), each of which is an attribute of godliness. Thus, as we acquire the gifts of the Spirit, made possible by the cleansing powers of the Atonement, we acquire the attributes of God.

Because of its expansive and comprehensive nature, the Atonement was referred to by certain Book of Mormon prophets as an "infinite atonement" (2 Nephi 9:7; 2 Nephi 25:16; Alma 34:10, 12).

It was infinite in *divineness* in that it was performed by the Holy One, the Only Begotten Son of God, who possessed every divine and godly attribute in unbounded measure (see D&C 109:77).

It was infinite in *power* in that the Savior was the only one who possessed the three powers necessary to save and exalt us—namely, the power to resurrect us from the dead, the power to redeem us from our sins, and the power to endow us with godly attributes (see John 11:25; Alma 12:15; Moroni 10:32–33).

It was infinite in *time*, both prospectively and retroactively (see Alma 34). As declared by King Benjamin, "Whosoever should believe that Christ should come, the same might receive remission of their sins . . . even as though he had already come among them" (Mosiah 3:13).

It was infinite in *coverage* since it provided the resurrection for all living things and, in addition, the opportunity for redemption and perfection for every person of every world of which the Savior was the creator (see D&C 76:23–24, 40–43).

It was infinite in *depth*—not only in whom it covered but also in what it covered. The Savior "descended below all things" (D&C 88:6), meaning He descended beneath all our sins so that even the "vilest of sinners" (Mosiah 28:4) and the "most lost of all mankind" (Alma 24:11) could be redeemed by His mercy. Further, His sacrifice descended beneath the total human plight, even that which has no relation to sin. Therefore, He comprehends the loneliness of the widow; He understands the agonizing parental pain when children go astray; and He can empathize with the excruciating pain of cancer and every other debilitating illness of man. As difficult as it might be to conceive, He, a perfect man, understands the rejections and weaknesses of mortals. There is no temporal condition, however ugly or gruesome it may seem, that has escaped His grasp. No one will be able to say at the judgment bar, "You did not understand my unique plight"—because He does. He "comprehendeth all things" (Alma 26:35) because He "descended below all things" (D&C 88:6). He not only has an infinite reservoir of redeeming powers but also an infinite reservoir of remedial powers. He not only redeems us from our worst sins but also has the power to remedy our smallest hurt or most insignificant weakness. He is the Master Healer, the Master Counselor, the

Master Comforter. There is no hurt He cannot soothe, no rejection He cannot assuage, no loneliness He cannot console, and no weakness He cannot strengthen. Whatever affliction the world casts at us, He has a remedy of superior healing power. His Atonement is infinite because it circumscribes and encompasses every finite condition known to mortals.

His Atonement is infinite in *suffering*. The Savior spoke of that awful, bitter cup, "which suffering caused myself, even God, the greatest of all, to tremble because of pain" (D&C 19:18). It commenced in Gethsemane, where in agony He bled from every pore, and concluded on Calvary, where He cried out, "My God, my God, why hast thou forsaken me?" (Matthew 27:46). He bore it all alone—the total human plight. His divine powers were not a shield to His suffering—to the contrary, when the pinnacle of pain would have triggered the release mechanism of death or unconsciousness in a mere mortal, the Savior summoned His divine powers, not to immunize Himself but to stay such relief mechanism until He had suffered the pain endured by every person of every world. Only then would He voluntarily lay down His life.

Finally, His Atonement was infinite in *love*—both the Son's and the Father's. The human mind cannot fully grasp such love. This is part of the sacredness and beauty of the event. It must be felt, not just reasoned. Someday we will understand that divine disclosure: "For God so loved the world, that he gave his only begotten Son" (John 3:16). Then, every knee will bow and every tongue confess that Jesus is the Christ.

The Savior is our only hope for salvation and exaltation. There is no "backup" man, alternative way, or contingency plan. As King Benjamin taught, "There shall be no other name given nor any other way nor means whereby salvation can come unto the children of men, only in and through the name of Christ, the Lord Omnipotent" (Mosiah 3:17).

In the process of His supreme sacrifice, the Savior satisfied every demand for justice and exercised every particle of mercy. He paid the awful price, the infinite price, to redeem us and perfect us. He is our Savior, our Redeemer, and our Exemplar.

The Atonement in a Spiritual Greenhouse

The doctrine of the Atonement is like a good seed planted in the ground. If, however, the seed is not nourished and taught in an atmosphere of spirituality, gratitude, and testimony, it will never bloom in the eye of the beholder. Sometimes the way we say something is as important as what we have to say.

When the Savior completed the Sermon on the Mount, "the people were astonished at his doctrine," and then the scriptures tell us why: "For he taught them as one having authority, and not as the scribes" (Matthew 7:28–29). Nephi gave the same prescription for effective teaching: "When a man speaketh by the power of the Holy Ghost the power of the Holy Ghost carrieth it unto the hearts of the children of men" (2 Nephi 33:1).

Some teachers may be caretakers or clock watchers until the class hour is completed; some may be entertainers; others are dispensers of factual information; some are motivators; and some are those never-to-be-forgotten teachers who are spiritual catalysts—those who speak with a power that not only momentarily motivates us to do good works but also permanently causes a change in our hearts. The doctrine of the Atonement thrives in such a spiritual climate—it is both sun and water in a single medium. There is no substitute for the Spirit—no other compensatory teaching technique. For only by the Spirit can the atoning doctrine come to full life.

Expressions of loving gratitude add to the nourishing of the seed. They break down defenses, cause meaningful reflection, and engender an atmosphere of humility and receptiveness to the truth. Who could listen to the touching words of gratitude expressed by Elder McConkie in his farewell sermon and not feel a kinship with the Savior and an eternal gratitude for His incomparable sacrifice: "I am one of his witnesses, and in a coming day I shall feel the nail marks in his hands and in his feet and shall wet his feet with my tears."[8]

Again and again the doctrine of the Atonement is accompanied by the power of testimony. Amulek boldly declared: "I say unto you, that I do know that Christ shall come among the children of men, to take upon him the transgressions of his people and that he shall atone for the sins of the world; for the Lord God hath spoken it" (Alma 34:8). Nowhere, however, is testimony more powerful than that expressed by the Savior Himself: "I have drunk out of that bitter cup which the Father hath given me, and have glorified the Father in taking upon me the sins of the world, in the which I have suffered the will of the Father in all things from the beginning" (3 Nephi 11:11). Testimonies such as these cause fire in our bones, cause our spirits to quake, and engrave the word of God upon our hearts.

In such an atmosphere as the foregoing, the prophets have issued life-changing challenges. It was Jacob who issued the towering challenge: "For why not speak of the atonement of Christ, and attain to a perfect knowledge of him?" (Jacob 4:12). As King Benjamin delivered his concluding sermon, he challenged his listeners: "If you believe all these things see that ye do them" (Mosiah 4:10). The response of his "spiritual students" was miraculous. They rejoiced "with such exceedingly great joy" and promised "we are willing to enter into a covenant with our God to do his will, and to be obedient to his commandments . . . all the remainder of our days" (Mosiah 5:4–5). What more could a teacher hope for?

Spirit, gratitude, testimony, and challenge—these are the nourishing agents of the spiritual greenhouse that allow the doctrine of the Atonement to thrive and blossom with radiant beauty. Teaching this doctrine requires the highest and best within us—our most creative powers, our most submissive spirit, and our finest intellectual faculties. For, in truth, it is the most profound, moving doctrine we will ever be privileged to teach.

Notes

1. This essay is a distillation of and reflection on the author's book, *The Infinite Atonement* (Salt Lake City: Deseret Book, 2000).
2. Bruce R. McConkie, "The Purifying Power of Gethsemane," *Ensign*, May 1985, 9.
3. Robert L. Millet, "Foreword," in Tad R. Callister, *The Infinite Atonement* (Salt Lake City: Deseret Book, 2000), ix.
4. Ezra Taft Benson, *A Witness and a Warning* (Salt Lake City: Deseret Book, 1988), 33.
5. Bruce R. McConkie, *A New Witness for the Articles of Faith* (Salt Lake City: Deseret Book, 1985), 467.
6. C. S. Lewis, *Mere Christianity* (New York: Collier Books, 1996), 129.
7. Ezra Taft Benson, *A Witness and a Warning* (Salt Lake City: Deseret Book, 1988), 18.
8. McConkie, "The Purifying Power of Gethsemane," 10.

Ever Learning, Ever Teaching: Lessons from Joseph F. Smith

David M. Whitchurch

David M. Whitchurch *is an associate professor of ancient scripture at BYU.*

When Carole Call King lost her mother (1986) and her father (1993),[1] she had no idea of the written legacy they had passed on to her. Actively involved in family history, she was given the family's genealogical records, but it would be three years before she discovered the significance of all she inherited. Somehow, the contents of one box were overlooked. Upon closer examination, she found hundreds of letters written to her great-grandmother Martha Ann Smith Harris, the daughter of Hyrum and Mary Fielding Smith. Among the letters were nearly a hundred written to Martha Ann from her brother, Joseph F. Smith, including an 1854 letter written from the Sandwich Isles that contained a lock of his hair.

This newly discovered treasure trove of letters provides a fresh and personal view into the lives of an early leader of The Church of Jesus Christ of Latter-day Saints and of his sister during a unique era of Church history. After the death of Mary Fielding Smith, the bond between her children was solidified and assuaged, to a small degree, through the medium of pen and paper. Seven decades of correspondence demonstrate the tremendous devotion between her children as they shared their innermost feelings, joys, heartaches, determinations, and family happenings. Their correspondence imparts a wealth of insights into the personal, caring nature of Joseph F. Smith and of the love he and his sister shared.

The letters range in dates from 1854, when Joseph F. Smith was a fifteen-year-old missionary in Hawaii, to 1916, just two years before his death. Additional Joseph F. and Martha Ann letters have been collected and added to those in the possession of Carole King. To date, 164 Joseph F. Smith and 48 Martha Ann Smith Harris letters have been collected and transcribed. The following chart summarizes the origin and number of letters sent.

Author	Location	Time Written	Quantity
Joseph F. Smith	Sandwich Isles	1854–58	12
	Nauvoo Legion Salt Lake City Area	1858	1
	European Mission/ British Isles Mission	1860–63	5
	Sandwich Isles	1864	1
	Salt Lake City	1865–74	30
	European Mission/ British Isles Mission	1874–75	9
	Salt Lake City	1876	2
	European Mission/ British Isles Mission	1877	1
	Salt Lake City	1877–84	19
	Exile/ Hiding in Sandwich Isles	1884–85	3
	Exile/Hiding—Possibly Washington, D.C. Area	1887–89	2
	Exile—Possibly Utah Area	1889–91	0
	Salt Lake City	1891–1918	79
	TOTAL		164
Martha Ann Harris	Salt Lake City	1854–67	26
	Provo	1867–1916	22
	TOTAL		48

A letter collection such as this provides multiple opportunities for researchers and interested historians to understand better the personal nature of Joseph F. Smith in the cultural/sociological framework of the early Church of Jesus Christ. The entire letter collection, along with its historical context, will be forthcoming in a book coauthored with Richard Neitzel Holzapfel.

This article will examine some of Joseph F. Smith's pedagogical methods as seen throughout his letters to Martha Ann. The categories and teaching methods are broad and yet somewhat limited—partially because of missing letters (especially those from Martha Ann Smith Harris) as well as difficulties of interpreting behavior changes through written correspondence. Nevertheless, the insights gained regarding Joseph F. Smith's personality and his talent as a teacher still provide considerable personal reflection and insight into his teaching capabilities. First, a brief background of Joseph F. Smith and his sister Martha Ann will be provided, followed by a general discussion on pedagogy. Finally, a small sampling of the letters themselves will be used to demonstrate some of Joseph F. Smith's teaching methods.

Background of Joseph Fielding (Joseph F.) Smith

In the spring and summer of 1836, Parley P. Pratt traveled in the vicinity of Toronto, Ontario, Canada, to preach the gospel of Jesus Christ as revealed to the Prophet Joseph Smith Jr.[2] Elder Pratt successfully arranged a meeting at a local farmhouse where a number of neighbors had gathered to hear his message. Included among his listeners was a man by the name of Joseph Fielding and "his two amiable and intelligent sisters," Mary and Mercy.[3]

Elder Pratt's message of the Restoration bore fruit, resulting in a number of baptisms, which included the Fieldings. Shortly after their conversion to the Church, Mary Fielding moved to Kirtland, Ohio, where she met and soon married the widower Hyrum Smith. Hyrum's wife, Jerusha Barden, had recently passed away, leaving him to care for their five children.[4]

Mary Fielding Smith's life was filled with hardship and trial. In the fall of 1838, persecution against the Church and its members forced Hyrum and his family to move from Kirtland, Ohio, to Far West, Missouri. On November 1, just two days after the Haun's Mill massacre, Hyrum, Joseph Smith Jr., and others were arrested and imprisoned. Their incarceration lasted nearly six months, leaving Mary Fielding to give birth to her firstborn child and care for Hyrum's five children without him. Joseph F. was born on November 13, 1838.[5]

Mary spent much of the next four months weak and bedridden. In January 1839, she traveled to Liberty, Missouri, in the back of a wagon so she and Joseph F. could visit Hyrum.

Continued harassment required Mary to move to Quincy, Illinois, in midwinter. After Hyrum's unexpected release from Liberty Jail, they left Quincy and moved to Commerce (Nauvoo), Illinois, where, for the next five years, they enjoyed a slight respite. It was during this lull that Mary gave birth to her second child, Martha Ann. She was born on May 14, 1841, in Nauvoo, Hancock County, Illinois.

In the spring and summer of 1844, the persecution against the Church again intensified. On June 27, Hyrum and Joseph Smith Jr. were martyred while jailed at Carthage, Illinois. Over the next two years, a series of events led to another exodus of the Saints. By the fall of 1846, Mary and her family left Nauvoo and moved to Winter Quarters (Florence), Nebraska, where they remained until the spring of 1848. Circumstances were such that when the family moved west with other migrating Saints, nine-year-old Joseph F. drove one of the family wagons to the Great Salt Lake Valley.[6] Four years after their arrival, Mary Fielding Smith died from illness brought about by exhaustion and lack of proper nutrition.

A year and a half after Mary Fielding Smith passed away, Joseph F.'s life took a dramatic turn. It was during the April 1854 general conference that President Brigham Young, speaking from the pulpit, read the names of those being called to serve missions for the Church. Without any previous inclination or advance notice, Joseph F. heard his name called as a missionary to go to the "Pacific Isles."[7]

The April 13, 1854, *Deseret News* reported the names of missionaries being sent to England, the United States, the Pacific Isles, Ireland, and British North America (that is, Canada). The *Deseret News* reported, "The following persons were then appointed and unanimously voted to go on missions, viz. . . . To the Pacific Isles: Orson Whitney, John Young (son of Lorenzo), Washington B. Rodgers, Simpson M. Molen, George Spiers [*sic*], Joseph Smith (son of Hyrum), Silas S. Smith (son of Silas), Silas Smith (son of Asahel), Sextus Johnson, John T. Caine."[8]

The difficulty and challenges of Joseph F.'s mission proved to be a superb training ground for his lifelong service in the Church. As previously mentioned, his time in the Pacific was also the beginning of an exchange of letters between himself and his sister. After nearly four years in the Sandwich Isles, he returned home in 1858 and joined the Nauvoo Legion in the Church's effort to thwart Johnston's army from coming into the Great Salt Lake Valley.[9]

Following a peaceful negotiation between Brigham Young and the United States government, Joseph F. Smith turned his attention to other matters, including marriage. On April 5, 1859, he married Levira Smith, a daughter of Samuel H. Smith. Other wives followed, including Julina Lambson (1866), Sarah Ellen Richards (1868), Edna Lambson (1871), Alice Ann Kimball (1883), and Mary Taylor Schwartz (1884). From these marriages came a total of forty-eight children.[10]

After serving two more missions, one to the British Isles and another to the Sandwich Isles, Joseph F. was called at age twenty-seven by Brigham Young as an Apostle and was named Second Counselor in the First Presidency.[11] A little over a year later, Joseph F. was set apart as a member of the Quorum of the Twelve Apostles. Joseph F. Smith's service as a counselor in the First Presidency continued under Presidents John Taylor and Lorenzo Snow. Passage of antipolygamy legislation and Joseph F. Smith's high profile caused him to go into exile and remain in hiding from August 1884 until President Benjamin Harrison granted him amnesty in the fall of 1891.[12]

On October 17, 1901, Joseph F. Smith was sustained as President of The Church of Jesus Christ of Latter-day Saints, where he served until his death at age eighty, passing away on November 19, 1918, in Salt Lake City.[13]

Brief Background of Martha Ann

Martha Ann Smith was born May 14, 1841, in Nauvoo, Illinois. Although we have less recorded history of her than we do her better-known brother, she must have endured the same trials as the rest of her family of living at Winter Quarters and of crossing the plains. After her mother's death, Martha Ann and Joseph F. moved in with a close family friend, Hannah Grinnells, where they remained until Hannah died a little more than a year later. Martha Ann then moved in with her mother's sister, Mercy Fielding Thompson.[14] Soon afterward, Joseph F. received his mission call to the Sandwich Isles. From the letters of Joseph F. and Martha Ann, it appears that Martha Ann also lived with Hyrum Smith and Jerusha Barden's son, John, prior to her marriage.

Heber C. Kimball married the fifteen-year-old Martha Ann to William Jasper Harris on April 21, 1857. Two days later, William left on a mission to the British Isles. Martha Ann moved in with her mother-in-law, Emily Harris

Smoot, the plural wife of Bishop Abraham O. Smoot.¹⁵ William returned home early from his mission in 1858 when missionaries were called from the mission field because of concerns over Johnston's army.

During the early summer of 1859, tragedy befell the Harris family. William was struck by lightning while plowing a field in Salt Lake City. Besides being badly burned, he was caught in the reins and dragged unconscious by runaway horses. Martha Ann nursed him back to health as best she could, but William never fully recovered, remaining weak for the rest of his life.

Eight years after this incident, Martha Ann and William moved to Provo with their five children. While in Provo, they added six more children to their family. The Harrises struggled financially much of their lives. William worked a variety of jobs. He served as a bodyguard for Brigham Young, worked in freighting, served as a policeman, and participated in mining activities.¹⁶ Martha Ann frequently supplemented the family income by sewing buckskin gloves and temple clothes.¹⁷ William Jasper Harris died on April 24, 1909, after being hit by a team of horses. His wife, Martha Ann, died October 19, 1923, at age eighty-three.

The Transcription Process

The primary objectives that guided the transcription of the Joseph F. Smith and Martha Ann Smith Harris letter collection were readability and accuracy. Transcriptions for each letter retain the original spelling, punctuation, superscripts, underlined words, and strike throughs whenever possible. The transcribers have done as little editing as possible, although minimal punctuation was added for clarity. To minimize reader distraction, we lowercased many letters that were written in capitals. For example, Martha Ann Smith Harris inconsistently used the capitals D, F, J, L, M, and S, and Joseph F.'s inconsistencies were most frequently seen in the letters A, J, L, M, and S. For readability purposes, editor discretion was used to standardize these letters.

Empty square brackets [ ] are used to represent a hole, tear, or otherwise missing portion of a letter. Broken words that begin on one line and finish on the next or words that end a line with a portion of the word written above or below it have been joined to read as a single word. Angle brackets < > are used for the original author's insertions. New paragraphs have been indented regardless of the page justification on the original letter. The symbol [—] was used to indicate unreadable letters within a word; [o] for one unreadable letter in a word; and "\" for a single word or series of words that could not be deciphered.

Pedagogy of Joseph F. Smith

After the passing of Mary Fielding Smith, circumstances dictated that Joseph F. function, in some regards, as both brother and parent to his younger sister. Not surprisingly, Martha Ann seems to have accepted the role of child as well as that of sister. She willingly listened to Joseph F.'s counsel and did her best to do what he asked. For example, from an extract of a letter written by Joseph F. (age seventeen) to Martha Ann (age fourteen) dated February 18, 1856, he wrote:

> Now then may I give you a little advice in regard how to act. Well the first is, do not seek to exalt yourself above your companions nor you must not try to act <u>refined</u> when you know nothing about refinement, but act stedy, mild, and be humble, meak and lowly in heart, and continually pray for the spirit of god to abide with you, for I tell you Martha Ann the spirit of god will Teach you the perfict rules of deacency, for it embodies no hypocracy, no superflues desines nor nothing of the sort, prayerfulness, humility, percivereance in righteousness, diligence, and long suffering combined will perfect us, and nothing els will enable us to attain to the glory and blessings prepaired for the faithful in the kingdom of God.

Although we do not presently have the corresponding letter to the one above, on numerous occasions, Martha Ann responded to his advice in a positive manner. In a letter dated sometime in the spring (likely April) of 1856—shortly after the above letter—she wrote:

> I receivd your letter and was glad to hear so kind and affectionate a letter it done me good to read it and it always does do me good to read a letter from you for I always learn something new that does me good. . . . I know what you want and and I will strive to do the best I can and the best I know how. I do not feel above taking your council but I want you [p. 2] to advise me what to do for you are older than I am and hav been tried mor than I hav. I consdder from whence your good advice comes I consider that it comes from a brother

who wishes me wel and who I had ~~rather re~~ as live receive advice from as any boddy in the world.

Throughout Joseph F.'s correspondence with his sister, it becomes increasingly evident that Martha Ann looked to him as a confidant, adviser, and mentor. Each of these words denotes teaching. The word *teacher* comes from Old English and means "to show the way (as in a person); to direct, conduct; or guide."[18]

Additional insights into the role of a teacher can be found if we examine its Greek counterpart *pedagogue*, from which the word *pedagogy* is derived. In the component parts of the word *pedagogue, pais* connotes "child" and *agoge* means "to lead out or away." When these terms are combined, the result suggests that pedagogy was originally concerned with the training of children. One scholar summarized the concept of pedagogy as "a temporarily defined process of intellectual and social development."[19]

When such definitions are applied to Joseph F. Smith, the result is his exemplification of an ideal teacher. Although he received little formal education and was only two and a half years older than Martha Ann, the death of their parents, his missionary experiences, and his ability to communicate seem to have placed him in the role of a teacher for Martha Ann. The techniques and principles discerned throughout his letters to her are much the same that modern educators espouse. Standards of effective teaching do not tire with age.

Numerous studies have examined quality teaching. At one time or another, surveys have been directed at groups such as school administrators, teachers, and students to examine the characteristics and traits of an ideal teacher. Educators James Banner and Harold Cannon reported, "Qualities that make for effective teaching are neither mysterious nor possessed by only a few exceptional instructors. They're inherent in all of us. One need not study those qualities so much as become aware of and employ them. . . . What teachers do cannot be distinguished from who they are."[20]

A similar case might be made for any good person—regardless of his or her education or chosen profession. A thoughtful examination of the apostles and prophets in our dispensation from Joseph Smith Jr. to Gordon B. Hinckley reveals individuals who have the ability—as stated earlier—to "direct, conduct; or guide"—in other words, to teach. Several studies were examined to help identify what makes a good teacher.[21] The lists generated from the various surveys were often too lengthy or unwieldy for the purposes of this paper.[22] Also included in many of the surveys were items such as fair grading, the encouragement of class discussion, suitable classroom environment, and classroom administration. Those deemed unsuitable for the circumstances of Joseph F. Smith and Martha Ann Smith Harris were eliminated. A shortened list was generated, and teaching traits were selected that were frequently reported as important in a majority of the studies examined.

The following five general teacher characteristics were identified and used to guide the rest of this article: (1) genuine concern or love for the persons being taught; (2) the ability to motivate; (3) the ability to communicate effectively; (4) the treating of others with respect; and (5) knowledge of the subject.

Genuine Concern or Love for the Persons Being Taught

> In Helen Keller's autobiography, she described the following incident:
>> The most important day I remember in all my life is the one on which my teacher, Anne Mansfield Sullivan, came to me. I am filled with wonder when I consider the immeasurable contrast between the two lives which it connects. It was the third of March, 1887, three months before I was seven years old. . . .
>>
>> I felt approaching footsteps. I stretched out my hand as I supposed to my mother. Some one took it, and I was caught up and held close in the arms of her who had come to reveal all things to me, and, more than all things else, to *love me*.[23]

Elder Dallin H. Oaks in a 1999 general conference address confirmed the essential ingredient of caring. He said, "A national author wrote a book about his greatest teacher. At the heart of this college teacher's powerful impact on his student was the student's conviction that this teacher really cared for him and wanted him to learn and do what would help him find happiness."[24] Martha Ann found such an individual in her brother. In the following letter that Joseph F. Smith wrote to his sister on June 22, 1864, he fondly reminisced about Hyrum, her ten-month-old son, and shared the great love he had for her and her family. The letter is written from the Sandwich Isles. Joseph F. had recently returned to Hawaii to help Elder Lorenzo Snow and other Church leaders respond to the apostate Walter Gibson.

My Dear Sister Martha Ann:— . . .

I sincerely hope that little Hyrum is better. I can hardly bear to think of seeing him changed in any way from his little, picture in my minde. I can always see him, streight and portly, strung up to the highest point of nerve, full of animation and life—& in a commanding manner & tone issuing weighty orders, that cannot be regarded lightly—or slighted with impunity, by the most majestic of his small but growing Empire! As he stands—in photograph—upon the tablet of my memory—he "is monarch of all he surveys," he knows no fear, no equel, he commands and—is obeyed, or woe! befall us!!! well he is my ideal—of male baby perfection! of genuine infantile nobility, & magnanimity!!

You well know I love the babies, they are all interresting to me from two months old, ~~and~~ upward. I wonder of Willie and Joseph will forget me, I guess not. kiss all of them for me, & tell them that I think of & pray for them ofton. that they may grow up—worthy of the great mercies of Him whos Image they so nobly bear. I think you have great cause to be proud of your boys. If they are not good men, it will not be their fault. The soil is your own, see that it lacks not cultivation.

In another letter written December 23, 1869, from Salt Lake City, Joseph F. expressed both encouragement and his desire to see Martha Ann. In this letter, he mentioned his second wife, Sarah, to whom he had been married for about a year. Only the last paragraph is quoted:

Martha Ann

My Dear Sister:— . . .

Sarah getting breakfast ready. I have dated this for tomorrow morning. Sarah gets things ready over night, and in the morning gets breakfast in 3/4 of an hour. I wish you could come and see us, and that I know how you are getting along. I have felt considerable anxiety for you, but I have not known how to avoid it, or in other words how to change fate. I feel condemned sometimes when I see the comfortable situation of my family and know that my own sister does not enjoy as much. I wish it were otherwise, but who can change it? Cheer up my sister something whispers to me it will not always be thus with <u>you</u>, and it <u>may</u> <u>not</u> <u>even</u> <u>with</u> <u>me</u>. There is allways a bright hope for the good, and a sure promis of reward. God bless you and yours. I will send you some paper and pens the first chance.

Although only two examples are provided of Joseph F.'s love for Martha Ann and her family, the letter collection offers ample evidence of a lifelong commitment to her—both in word and deed. King Benjamin's words find a fitting example in Joseph F. Smith as Martha Ann's surrogate parent, as he heeded the counsel that parents are to care for their children and "teach them to love one another, and to serve one another" (Mosiah 4:14–15). Besides expressions of praise, encouragement, and love, the letter collection indicates that Joseph F. frequently provided monetary help to his sister. His willingness to share becomes more remarkable when we consider the economic challenges he faced in meeting the needs of his own large family.

The Ability to Motivate and to Communicate Effectively

The delineation between motivation and communication can be difficult to assess, especially since effective communication is so integral to pedagogy. Joseph F. Smith's letters and his ability to communicate stand on their own merit. His success and his ability to motivate others are grounded in effective communication skills.

Motivation manifests itself in many ways. Whether it be money, prestige, or the need to belong, motivation is typified in change. This change can be brought about by simple factors such as thirst on a hot summer's day. How much is ice-cold water worth? It often depends on how thirsty the potential customer is. Another powerful motivator of change is love. The scriptures simply state, "If you love me, keep my commandments" (John 14:15). One author put it this way: "We work hard and go that extra mile for those we love."[25] Studies have shown that students who like their teachers are much more likely to work harder and perform better than those who don't.

In responding to the question, "What does good teaching involve?" Robert Leamnson, author of *Thinking about Teaching and Learning*, stated, "I see the major elements as exposing, and inspiring."[26] Joseph F. Smith adeptly addressed areas that he felt Martha Ann needed to improve on. There is little question about Martha Ann's love and commitment to her older brother. How much influence his counsel had on her is impossible to measure; yet, because of her love for him, we can assume only that Martha Ann carefully listened to her older brother and responded as best she could. For example, when Joseph F. was just sixteen years old, he penned from the Island of Maui the following letter (dated January 28, 1855) to his thirteen-year-old sister, encouraging her to live a life worthy of God's blessings. Still displaying his youth and lack of formal education, he wrote:

> My Dear and affectionate <Sister> Martha.
>
> Haveing jest finished writing a letter to Jerusha. I thought that I would try and write one to you also thinking that a fiew lines from me would be acceptibal to you. I am well and Harty. and Have grew conciderable since you saw me last and I have no reasons to doubt but what you have grew much larger you ware when I last saw you. if you have you Have got to be quiet a woman and I supose that you have got so that you can look over the heds of your Sisters. and now I would like to give you some little council, if you will take it and that is this. be Humbel and prayorful, and be kind to your connections and you will Have the Spirit of the Lord abiding with you at all times and the lord will bless you and you will give up in the footsteps of your Mother and you will be blessed with every thing even as your Mother was. and you will neve[ ] lack for the comforts of life if you will only growe up in the footstep[ ] of our Mother who has gon before us. only be kind to your Sisters and mind what they say to you and never git above them for they are your older Sisters, and it is for them to give council and also for our oldest Brothers. you be kind to them and do what they and donot get cross. and study your books. and stop at home as much as posible and do not think because you have not the priveliges of meny that you are slited but be sober and prayorful, and you will groe up in the footsteps of our Mother. and I would rather groe up in the ways of my Mother than to have all the riches in this world, and be wild and rude, and unprayorful. for if you groe up after your Mother you will never lack for the comforts of life. I will ask you a question. did you ever know the time when we were not provided for by the Hand of our Mother [p. 2] I answer, the time never was known. <u>ask those who knows</u>. I could give you

much council <u>Moty</u>, that would be benifissial to you as long as you live upon this earth. Only remember what I have alredy sed and se if it will not be good in days to come. I must now bring my letter to close. Preying the Lord to bless you and prosper you all the day long. and I want you to write to me as often as you can and let me know how you are giting along.

One thing more never feel down harted but be merry <in your hart,> and joyful. and keepe a prayorful hand and a thoughtful mind and the Lord will L <u>Bless you</u>.

This particular letter demonstrates the tremendous love and esteem Joseph F. held for his mother as well as his personal recognition of the many sacrifices she made for her family. His reference to their mother must have been compelling to a young Martha Ann as she grappled with the challenges of her older siblings (Hyrum and Jerusha's children) and the insecurities that would naturally accompany the loss of her parents and separation from her brother.

Another means of motivation comes from sharing personal experience. Stories tend to elicit feelings of tenderness and endearment that, in turn, motivate change. Advertisers often use stories to create feelings of acceptance or need. For years, the Church has used a series of short radio and television spots that capture unique family moments to elicit feelings of reflection on the importance of family. The spots usually end with the catch phrase, "Family—isn't it about . . . time?"

On numerous occasions, the scriptures use stories to teach and motivate. On one occasion, while traveling through Samaria, Jesus stopped at a well in Sychar and spoke with a woman who had come to draw water (see John 4). During His conversation with her, He said, "If thou knewest the gift of God, and who it is that saith to thee, Give me to drink; thou wouldest have asked of him, and he would have given thee living water" (4:10). Their exchange led Him to testify of His divinity. Many of Jesus's teaching moments were prompted by circumstances or events—for example, the cursing of the fig tree (see Matthew 21:19–22), His disciples' plucking and eating grain on the Sabbath (see Mark 2:23–28), and the healing of the woman with an eighteen-year infirmity (see Luke 13:11–17).

Joseph F. Smith also used current events and personal experiences to teach God's providence in his life. Such examples likely helped motivate Martha Ann to live a life worthy of such blessings. Two such examples are provided below. The first comes from a letter written April 17, 1857, from Lahaina, Sandwich Islands. An eighteen-year-old Joseph F. eloquently communicated two personal experiences to his fifteen-year-old sister:

My Dear Sister Martha Ann:—

It is with no ordinary feeling that I seat myself this morning to reciprocate your favor of December 17th '56, it graced my presence on the 28th ultimo, but I have had no oppertunity of answering it untill now, owing to my travels to Conference, &c. which came off on the 7th, 8th and 9th of this month. We had a good time togather. I am well and hearty at the present, altho' I feel verry sore and and dull this morning becaus of sleeplessness, and labor for the last three days and nights

Eight of us started from the Island of Lanai on Wednesday, and on acount of contrary and high winds we ware compelled to return to port, here we slept out doors with nothing but a verry thin mat for a bead, and another one for a covering, our carpet-sacks serving for pillows, at <u>moon rise</u> in the morning, (1 o clock) we went on board of our little Boat and started for this Island. Martha it would make you wonder if you could see us being tossed and driven by the waves of the mighty Paciffic, when every wave seemed like it was the next moment going to engulf us in t̶h̶e̶ its auful surge, yes, to see us in an open Boat, with a tract of Ocean before us of some 15 miles, and only a <u>one fourth inch</u> of pine boards between us and the tremenduous, dreadful, yawning <u>grave</u> of thousands of poor ill-fated beings, who ware not so fortunate as ourselves; when you get with in a quarter of an inch of death itself, then who can save you? Marth, the <u>arm</u> on which we trusted is that which hath delivered, it is ever willing to deliver, and <u>will</u> deliver all who lean upon it, and put all their trust on it, therefore lets be faithful. [p. 2] Well, we arived at this place, at 10 o clock in the morning of the next day, after we started.—and this morning several of the Brethren started for Wailuku leaving three of us at this place. I have been appointed to preside over the Molokai, conference, which is about 15 miles from this place, and on another Island, so you see I have to cross another strip of Ocean before I get to my field of labor. When we arived at this place we found that 33.50$ of money recieved for Books of Mormon, that has been solde to the Native Saints had been <u>stolen</u>, who the perpetrator of this dead was, we are at loss to know or finde out. certain, it is we are in distress because of it, and that any person who would take money from <u>us</u>, who knew our situation, is wors than a <u>murderor</u>! but it seems that the Devil exerts his utmoste power to thwart every thing that we attempt to do for the prosperity and emelioration of this people. the Lord only knows what will take place next. to impede his moste holy work, who could endure what we have to, but mormon Elders? I do not believe, that man lives outside of the kingdom of God that would <u>begin</u> to endure to allmoste indurable trials and privations that seem to beset us on every hand, and that we have to pass thro' evry day of our lives on these degraded lands, yet it is all for the best. I feel to rejoice, Martha, all the day long. I feel buoyant & hopeful, and like pressing forward, notwithstanding the hardships I have to encounter, because I know what I am doing, and for whom I am laboring, it is not as though I was seaking for gane, or secularly striving for the vain things of this world. if it was so, no one could have escaped despondancy, provided this was his dernier <prospects> for [p. 3] advancement.—

Perspectives gained through sharing personal trials and experiences often enhance a person's ability to deal with life's difficulties. Consider the inspiration and perspective the Old Testament story of Job has had on its readers. With no way of measuring the impact of Joseph F. Smith's letters on Martha Ann, we may never realize just how influential they really were for her; yet the stories and lessons shared in his letters should not be overlooked. Quality teaching requires an investment of self—a sharing from the heart. The strength and effectiveness of Joseph F.'s letters come, in part, through his conveyance of his extraordinary circumstances. Most teachers anticipate that by sharing such personal experiences, they will influence their students to strive toward some greater good. Hopefully, Martha Ann's newly acquired perspective from her brother's letters influenced her in a similar manner.

Another letter of Joseph F. provides a look at how the weather and the two-month anniversary of the passing of his firstborn child triggered memories of early childhood events. Joseph F. was thirty-one years old at the time as he reminisced about Mercy Josephine, his daughter with Julina Lambson Smith. Mercy Josephine was less than ten months old at her passing:

> City, Aug. 6th. 1870
>
> Martha Ann
>
> My Dear Sister:— . . .
>
> The weather is very oppressive, and the atmosphere sultry and merky, as tho' impregnated with smoke. Much as it was on the days memorable as the 27th, of June 1844. And the 21st. and 22nd of Sept. 1852—the day of fathers death, and the death and burial of Mother, I recollect them distinctly. It is two months to day since my own sweet babe joined her grand father and mother in the spirit world, leaving in my hearts affections a <u>void</u> and broken space that time nor earth can ever fill. I mourn the earthly loss of the brightest, purest, dearest, treasure God ever gave me. the one, I prized and cherished most, within the great circle of that greatest gift of God "Eternal Life", [p. 2] which is incomparable, being "All in All," and yet as if to compensate in some degree, for my bereavement, fresh sweetness and beauty, increasing inteligence, and love daily developes in my precious, cheerful, merry little "rose bud", left me to bloom and blossom in my cottage "alone." O! in the midst of sorrow, I can say, I thank God for my three sweet, perfect little gifts, "<u>one</u> on earth and <u>two</u> in heaven", the centre of my love, my own sweet "Jode". The fountain of my tears has never closed when I have permitted them to flow, but I complain only of my own weakness and ignorance.

Martha Ann's own sympathetic ear must have been stirred as she read her brother's letter. Presumably, she wrote Joseph F. of her own worries about her children (unfortunately, this letter is not included in our collection). Whatever Martha Ann wrote to him, he responded to her letter with his own letter dated August 18, 1870:

> The Lord says he will have a "tried people", all that [p. 2] is dross must sooner or later be consumed, for only the "gold" will remain. I hope for the sake of <u>parantage</u> as well as for <u>our</u> own sake, and the sake of our children, we may be proven to be the <u>pure</u> <u>mettal</u>. I must say that Mormonism, or the Gospel

in all its parts grows brighter and brighter with me, & this will inevitably be the case the more it is <u>rubbed</u>, and the Devil and all his <u>imps</u> seem bent on polishing us <it> up. There is one consolation, that is, the wicked can do nothing <u>against</u>, but <u>for</u> the cause of truth. My family are <u>well</u>, [ ]y has had several [ ]s of diarhea but nothing serious. Julina is very careful, "burnt child dreads the fire", we dread sickness or even the slightest illness of baby. O! may God spare here for <u>my sake</u>.

Joseph F. Smith seems to have drawn strength and resolve from his knowledge of gospel principles. His very faith reflects his understanding. Measuring motivation is difficult, especially as observed through personal correspondence written so long ago. Even so, Joseph F.'s passion and earnest entreaties conveyed through this letter disclose his feelings of compassion and an understanding of why misfortune and heartache occur. Although we may never know how his letters motivated or helped Martha Ann deal with the hardships of early western living, their capacity to comfort and provide her with new perspective to meet those challenges is readily visible in his writings.

The Treating of Others with Respect

Another element of effective teaching is the ability to respect those whom teachers teach. Teachers need to recognize that they often learn as much from their students as they teach them—that is, teaching is a two-way street. Effective teachers demonstrate respect for their students as the teachers listen and interact with the students. Parker Palmer, in an article entitled "The Heart of a Teacher: Identity and Integrity in Teaching," stated:

> Teaching, like any truly human activity, emerges from one's inwardness, for better or worse. As I teach, I project the condition of my soul onto my students, my subject, and our way of being together. The entanglements I experience in the classroom are often no more or less than the convolutions of my inner life. Viewed from this angle, teaching holds a mirror to the soul. If I am willing to look in that mirror, and not run from what I see, I have a chance to gain self-knowledge—and knowing myself is as crucial to good teaching as knowing my students and my subject.[27]

The Savior demonstrated this principle when traveling in the area of Tyre and Sidon (see Mark 7:24–30). While He was there, a non-Israelite woman pleaded with Him to heal her unclean daughter. Jesus responded by saying, "Let the children first be filled: for it is not meet to take the children's bread, and to cast it unto the dogs" (7:27). In essence, He was telling her His mission was not to the Gentiles and that He would not heal her daughter. Not satisfied, the woman reminded the Savior that even household pets receive bread from their master's table. After hearing her, Jesus responded by healing her daughter. For teaching to be genuine, students need to know that teachers do listen and respond accordingly. Joseph F. Smith demonstrates his own willingness to listen to Martha Ann in the following letter:

> Sandwich Islands
>
> June 14, 1857. . .
>
> Dearest Sister. one short sentence in your letter, struck me like the mighty surge of Occeans tempestuous swell! what was it?— "I feel that I am a weak and frail being—& why should not God bless you, who is much more worthy than I am, for, he has blessd me"—martha, do not tempt me. that language, tho' simple—speaks louder than the bolts of Heaven, that you do love me. and that you do desire to live humbe, and prayerful. Oh! humility! how beutious are thy influences. how profoundly, deep thy serenity and bliss! this subject, <u>subdews</u>—it <u>melts</u> me!—<u>Martha</u> what you said admonished me. I kindely accept its chastening influance, although quite undirected. when I read it something seemed to whisper gently in my minde, <u>Joseph</u>? "understandest thou what thou readeth"? "let him that readeth understand", these th admonishing thoughts came to my minde with the words, "wake up more fully to your duty!" I can look back and see where I might have bettered my course. where I might have been more dilegent in descharge of my duty. but then, these thoughts are dispelled by the strictly varacious adage "time once past never will return, the moment lost, is lost for ever"! therefore why morne for things we cannot help. or in the words of Dear [p. 2] Cousin Josephine, why, "sigh o'er the plesures now faided. And the joys time can never restore?" there is no use, I am fully resolved to take things as they come, and as they fleet along by with [ ] unchangible goings of time, I feel

to say, farewell, thou hurring time. thou industrious time, that wateth not for the sluggard, neither can man stay thy speading progress. but do thy duty in hastening the period when all creation shall reach the end for which they were created.

Martha Ann's mild rebuff became an opportunity for Joseph F. to examine his heart and make some course corrections in his own life. The *Oxford English Dictionary* defines *respect* as follows: "to treat or regard with deference, esteem, or honor."[28] Effective teachers demonstrate deference for their students by listening to them and making appropriate changes. Teachers who lack respect for their students may do so for the following reasons:

First, teachers may mistakenly believe that listening to their students somehow makes teachers vulnerable to additional criticism (that is, if it worked once, it might work again).

Second, teachers might be afraid to expose their personal weaknesses to their students because doing so shows that teachers do make mistakes and really do not have all the answers. In reality, however, the drawbacks of such thinking far exceed the benefits. Students who see the humanity in their teachers are much more likely to reciprocate in their responses to teacher demands and expectations. Parker Palmer provides some insight into those teachers who open themselves up to their students:

> As good teachers weave the fabric that joins them with students and subjects, the heart is the loom on which the threads are tied: the tension is held, the shuttle flies, and the fabric is stretched tight. Small wonder, then, that teaching tugs at the heart, opens the heart, even breaks the heart—and the more one loves teaching, the more heartbreaking it can be.
>
> We became teachers for reasons of the heart, animated by a passion for some subject and for helping people to learn. . . . The courage to teach is the courage to keep one's heart open in those very moments when the heart is asked to hold more than it is able, so that teacher and students and subject can be woven into the fabric of community that learning, and living, require.[29]

Another letter that demonstrates Joseph F.'s respect for his sister can be seen in an exchange of letters on marriage. On May 3, 1857, Martha Ann wrote to her brother to tell him she was married. She was just two weeks from her sixteenth birthday and wrote with some concern as to how Joseph F. would respond:

> B Dear b<rother> I have an itam of news to write to you and my hand trembles when I go to write it for my concence is gilty before my brother for I fear that he will think I have slited him but for give me dear brother if I say that I have \ but I fear that it will dampen your feelings but I can not help it now I must say it enny how I am married—to William harris. I suppose that this will shock you to hear \ <it>, it almost shocks me to thnk of it my sellf when I thnk of it but it is really sow now I must tell you the whis and the whare fors and then I hope you wll not blame me so much he had been keepping companey with me John[30] gave him leave to do so and I had no objection to it and ~~my~~ I began to think considderable of him and he began to think considerrabe of me. to tell the of the matter my \ thaughts has been that way for some time for 2 years at the least and my mind has not been among studys as you can plainly se my ~~mind~~ heart was young and tender and I let it go to far and John notesed it for I did not tell it to enny boddy not even to you who was my nearest and dearst friend and I tr<i>ed to concal my all could \ but John found it out in site of me [p. 3] for he could se that I did not learn much and he had to know the resoning and I had to tell him and \ John went to brother kimbol[31] about it and he said that we had better git married be fore he went away and John thaught that it would \ be the best and then my mind would be setteld and then I could learn some thing but other wse I could not. and ~~wll~~ william went up to git his parting blesings and I did not know for certain that I should git married befor he went away. and brother Kimible sent him after me and told \ him that he had better ~~git~~ have it all done up that day and he came and I went and was seald over the alter. and he started to ingland ~~to drag~~ on a mission to drag a hand cart acrosst the plains we was married on tusday and he started on thursdas

so you see that I did not stop long with him and I am glad of it for if he had not have going to away money could not have herd me to have ben married untll you come home for I have long wished for your <re>turn with a longing heart that I mght be the same when you come back as I was when you went away. but allas things can not be just as the huane heart would desire. I am just the same as I was onely I am married I will be free for three years yet. and dear brother I beseach of you to ~~is~~ treat me as you always did if you dont it will almost break my heart give me council and I wil try to abid it I am not perfect yet and I shall thank you for your council<cil> and I am not ofended to you if I was I thinks I would ~~be~~ be a fool \ and would need castisements for it I am thankful to my [p. 4] father for giving me a brother that cears for mya. wefare for I know that you care for my welfarre more than enny boddy else can ~~feel~~ <care> fore upon this irth O Joseph would to god that I could expres feellings just as they are and \ I express my thanks to you for your kindnes to me. I can never for git you for ever no not for an hour I have never forgotts you senc you left me to far away from your home. I have thaught of you in what ever place I have been no matter whare.

On June 14, 1857, Joseph F. wrote a letter to Martha Ann before receiving the above letter. Interestingly, Joseph F., not knowing that Martha Ann had married William Harris, wrote a letter that addressed the topic of marriage. A brief excerpt from it provides the tone:

. . . well, now am I bound to any one? No, I am not. is any one bound to me, by her sacred <u>vows</u> for life No, there are non. now what is the reason?— I will reveal the secret. I have <u>not</u> my life ensured, only by my own <u>goodness</u>, my own true merrit. then God will, or has ensured my life to enjoy many great blessings. therefor if I am spaired to join my life with <u>one</u> in whome there is a spark of heavenly fire, that beams and blazes in the dark hour of adversity and that is willing to shair the humble lot of One whome God knows loves the humble and honest heart. then I will say to God be the glory, what <u>hour</u> is mine? what moment is my own? at what time may God say, Joseph, thy soul is required of thee—? can I say no? I

> cannot, then I say thank the Lord no soul is bownd to mine at stake of houer. varasity, and vertue, no, I am free as the air, so ~~are~~ <is> avery one free from me, I wish to be tied to no one till I am able to provide and take care of her, untill then <u>hear ye O—fair ones, ye are free from me,</u>—where no <u>vows</u> are made no hearts are broken. now the whole amount of this is, when sumed up. I do not want you to make any vows, with any one if you can avoid it. . . .

We can only wonder exactly how Joseph F. initially responded to Martha Ann's news, knowing that he did not want her to get married yet. The letter he wrote to her helps demonstrate his capacity to respect Martha Ann. The following letter was written on July 25, 1857:

> Dear Sister Martha Ann:—I recieved your long letter of May 3rd—about a week ago, and was verry glad indeed to hear from you; I was somwhat surprised on hearing of your marriage. but as I was not there to partisipate in the ~~in the~~ scene, I can only wish you much joy;—and happy life You have now taken the moste important step of your life—or existance—under the Bonds of the Gospel. upon the step you have just taken is pending all the social enjoyments—and happiness of your present existance—and the Blessings of a happy and chearful home. as well as an obediant and God-like posterity,—<u>or</u> the misories and heart-rending scenes: of discontent,—discord & bitter unhappiness;—I almoste quake when I think upon this all obsorbing subject—to the center. when I look around me and reflect upon the many <u>direful</u> circumstanses accuring from day to day,—among the great and the Learned, the Small and the Ignorant, as well as the Rich and the Poor;—of "heart-Broken" women, distracted husbands, "Jealousy" in all its hideous formes—suspicion with all his train of poisonous rancour. with his drawn daggar and un-cheathed vengense. ready to spill the <u>hearts Blood</u> of "Wives", "Husbands", & "Children"! I shrink with horro<u>r from the scene:— It does seem curious in the extreem to me, why folks go so head-long into business that so greatly concerns their future prosperity and happiness on the other hand will bring down upon them ponderous grieveancies, and a world of truble,—from

which they may never extract themselvs—and inverriably a Bad name—however—with all these conciderations—before us—it is not with us, as it is with the World at Learge—we have the the light of the Gospel the—influance of the Holy Spirit—the teachings of the Prophits & servants of God, to "Lead us into all truth" and teach us our duty— If you have adhered to counsel—it is all right—and you will come off victorioous. You will certainly leave off Girl-ism now. I hope you will remem[p. 2]ber your possition, and let your actions and conduct in all things, and at all times be such as will store up for you Respect, Esteem, and Friendship in the heart of every honest and good person. now, do you want me to tell you the way to attain to this desireable possition?—prayer—with faith, and hope on Jesus and his Gospel, will alone do it. a person that holdes your stateon in the True Kingdom of God, need never fear the face of "Clay."

Rather than chastise or condemn Martha Ann for getting married, Joseph F. demonstrates his maturity by wishing her joy and happiness followed with gentle and kind counsel. His respect for his sister is even more remarkable when we consider he was just eighteen years old at the time he wrote this letter. Effective teachers recognize where their students are in life and, rather than judge them harshly for decisions they make, turn life's circumstances into opportunities to teach. The doctrinal insights Joseph F. Smith shared in the latter portion of this letter demonstrate just how much gospel knowledge he had gained at such a young age. Throughout his life, he used this knowledge to bless others.

Knowledge of the Subject

Joseph F. Smith's lifelong commitment to knowledge and his practical talent to share it resonate throughout his letters to Martha Ann. Solomon stated, "Wisdom is the principal thing; therefore get wisdom: and with all thy getting get understanding" (Proverbs 4:7). The latter half of this poetic couplet suggests that wisdom requires knowledge. The dictionary corroborates this assertion, as its definition comprises words like "practical knowledge" or "understanding."[32]

Few would argue that teaching requires at least a limited amount of knowledge, but most realize and fully recognize that *effective* teaching—the kind that brings about real change—demands wisdom. President Boyd K. Packer said, "I have long believed that the study of the doctrines of the gospel will improve behavior quicker than talking about behavior will improve behavior."[33]

From the time that Joseph F. Smith left on his mission, he demonstrated a precocious understanding of the Restoration and its truths; with this knowledge, he sought to bless others by bringing positive change into their lives. Although his life was filled with many hardships and heartaches, he must have taken great delight in testifying of Jesus Christ and the truths of the restored gospel. At just sixteen years of age, he wrote the following letter to Martha Ann from Maui, Sandwich Isles, on June 9, 1855:

> My Dear and affectionate
> Sister, Martha Ann. . . .
> . . . be a Mormon out, and out, and you will be pl blessed, I find that thare is nothing that will try a person so as to tell this world that he is a mormon, but I feel first rate. I am fat, and stout, I feel like I could through all the hays down that thare is in the valeys. (but I donot know how it would be if I should try it)
> I am a Preaching (Marty) like a good one, (you had aught to here me) or (or my voys, (I suppose if you wase any whare nee the Islands you could) we had a good meeting this morning, and I was caled upon to Preach, I acordingly, made an attempt.

As Joseph F's enthusiasm and ability to teach the gospel matured, he also learned to take personal comfort in his knowledge and conviction of the plan of salvation. In a letter dated August 26, 1883, he wrote from Salt Lake City following the death of his son, Albert Jesse Smith:[34]

> My Dear sister Martha Ann,
> Once more, and now for the sixth time, by the inexorable will of an inscrutable providence we have been called upon to part with one of our dearest, most preacious treasures.
> This time the pitiless monster, death, has chosen for his "shining mark" our beautiful, inteligent, bright and lovely little Albert Jesse. His death occurred yesterday at 11.35 a.m. after an illness of about 13 days, most of which time I was absent from home, travelling thro' the settlements north with

Pres. Taylor. I arrived home on thursday morning having been sent for, and being honorably released by the President. I had the [p. 2] sorrowful pleasure of watching and waiting upon him, my darling boy, for 52 hours, with heart-felt prayers and scalding tears not a few, but the heavens were brass over our heads. our crys and tears fell alike to the earth and all were buried this day with the lifeless, beautious form of our hearts' treasure in the grave! and yet not all were buried, for still our cry <u>would</u> assend, why is it so? O. God why had it to be? and still our tears seak the earth to releave if not to bury our heartaches in its feelingless bosom.

If for the sorrows of parting with our little, innocent ones in this world, we are to be rewarded with joy in the near or distant future, then may I not hope for a rich reward hereafter! Have I not laid up treasures in heaven? Sarah Ella, Mercy Josephine, Heber John, Alfred Jason, Rhoda Ann, and now Albert Jesse, all hold out their loving arms to "Papa," from the other side. What a happy meeting awaits me! and I trust, that in that ransomed [p. 3] throng no hearts nor hands will welcome me more warmly than those of Father, <u>Mother</u>, Hyrum, Mary, (whom we knew not) and Sarah,[35] and Lovina,[36] and hosts of Kindred dead who being "dead yet live", they having tasted of the living waters of christ, and died in Him. By far the greatest number are beyond the vail, the ties which draw us thither are fast becoming stronger than those which bind us here. Yet I look upon my little flocks now drawing upon me for their daily food, and none in store, but trusting in providence, and depending upon my mortal life for <their> help and protection and I breathe the earnest prayor, O! let me stay to battle with the ills and ups and downs of life yet a little longer in the world for their dear sakes. Were it not for this, now while my soul is cleansed by poignant grief I would rather go than stay. and yet I half feel that I am neither good enough to go or stay. It seemes not [p. 4] always an easy task to acknowledge the hand of God in <u>All</u> things. yet I <u>will</u> do it. and my heart says, "tho' He slay me yet will I trust in Him,"[37] for "The Lord giveth and the Lord taketh away, blessed be the

name of the Lord."[38] I would rather have to pass through the the scenes of the past few days, harrowing as they have been, to the heart and soul, time and time again than never to have had my precious boy. Our aim can be no higher or nobler than to aspire to <u>be worthy</u> of an eternal union with, and possession of the pure, innocent trusting and loving little souls, such as those with whom God has blessed me only for so such short and happy periods of time. God help us to be worthy of them.
Joseph

Any parent naturally feels the loss and pain that accompany the death of a child. Through that loss, Joseph F. Smith's knowledge of the gospel provided hope and a determination to live worthily so he could be reunited with his family in the life to come. Few dimensions of the gospel hold more importance. We do not know how Martha Ann reacted to her brother's grief; yet we can suppose that she, too, felt the sorrow and hopeful resolve to live a life worthy of eternal reunion.

Conclusion

Joseph F. Smith's pedagogical talent provides an ideal example of what teachers can and should be. As indicated earlier, the standards of effective teaching do not tire with age. Although a limited number of teaching traits and characteristics were explored in this paper, Joseph F. Smith's letters confirm his capacity to teach as he helped direct, conduct, and guide Martha Ann in her intellectual, social, and spiritual progress. His letters clearly show that his depth of gospel knowledge, along with his profound ability to love, respect, motivate, and communicate effectively, were an integral part of Martha Ann's development.

The greatest explanation for Joseph F. Smith's teaching success may simply be that he was a successful person who loved God and did all in his power to bless the lives of those around him. No less should be expected from any disciple of Jesus Christ. The charge given by Elder Jeffrey R. Holland regarding teachers helps remind us all of our duty to be effective teachers:

> Now, at a time when our prophet is calling for more faith through hearing the word of God, we must revitalize and reenthrone superior teaching in the Church—at home, from the pulpit, in our administrative meetings, and surely in the classroom. Inspired teaching must never become a lost art in

the Church, and we must make certain our quest for it does not become a lost tradition. . . .

When crises come in our lives—and they will—the philosophies of men interlaced with a few scriptures and poems just won't do. Are we really nurturing our youth and our new members in a way that will sustain them when the stresses of life appear? Or are we giving them a kind of theological Twinkie—spiritually empty calories? President John Taylor once called such teaching "fried froth," the kind of thing you could eat all day and yet finish feeling totally unsatisfied. . . .

Whether we are instructing our children at home or standing before an audience at church, let us *never* make our faith difficult to detect. Remember, we are to be teachers "come from God." . . . Give scripturally based sermons. Teach the revealed doctrine. Bear heartfelt testimony.[39]

Notes

1. Her mother, Verna Passey Call, died October 8, 1986, and her father, Anson Bowen Call Jr., died on June 1, 1993.
2. Parley P. Pratt, *Autobiography of Parley P. Pratt* (Salt Lake City: Deseret Book, 1985), 110.
3. Pratt, *Autobiography*, 128.
4. Francis M. Gibbons, *Joseph F. Smith: Patriarch and Preacher, Prophet of God* (Salt Lake City: Deseret Book, 1984), 1–2.
5. In Daniel H. Ludlow, ed., *Encyclopedia of Mormonism* (New York: Macmillan, 1992), 3:1350.
6. Ludlow, *Encyclopedia of Mormonism*, 3:1350.
7. Gibbons, *Joseph F. Smith*, 27.
8. *Deseret News*, April 13, 1854.
9. Gibbons, *Joseph F. Smith*, 45–46.
10. Ludlow, *Encyclopedia of Mormonism*, 3:1352.
11. Gibbons, *Joseph F. Smith*, 87.
12. Gibbons, *Joseph F. Smith*, 130–32, 181–82.
13. Ludlow, *Encyclopedia of Mormonism*, 3:1352.
14. Sarah Harris Passey, *History of Martha Ann Smith Harris*, unpublished manuscript, 4; Sarah Harris Passey is a daughter.

15. Carole Call King, *History of William Jasper Harris, 1836–1909*, unpublished manuscript, 2; Carole Call King is a great-granddaughter.
16. King, *History of William Jasper Harris*, 5–6.
17. Passey, *History of Martha Ann Smith Harris*, 5–6.
18. *Oxford English Dictionary*, 2nd ed., version 2.0, s.v. "teach" (Oxford: Oxford University Press: 1999).
19. Yun Lee Too, *The Pedagogical Contract* (Ann Arbor, MI: University of Michigan Press, 2000), 123.
20. James M. Banner Jr. and Harold C. Cannon, "The Personal Qualities of Teaching," *Change* 29, no. 6 (November/December 1997): 43.
21. For example, see Teresa Pica, Gregory A. Barnes, and Alexis Gerard Finger, *Teaching Matters: Skills and Strategies for International Teaching Assistants* (New York: HarperCollins, 1990), 166–67; Banner and Cannon, "The Personal Qualities of Teaching," 40; Gary Gordon, "Teacher Talent and Urban Schools," *Phi Delta Kappan* 81, no. 4 (December 1999): 4; Peter G. Beidler, "What Makes a Good Teacher," in *Inspiring Teaching*, ed. John K. Roth (Boston: Anker, 1997).
22. Banner and Cannon, "The Personal Qualities of Teaching," 43.
23. Helen Keller, *The Story of My Life* (Norwalk, CT: Easton Press, 1988), 21–22; emphasis added.
24. Dallin H. Oaks, "Gospel Teaching," *Ensign*, November 1999, 78.
25. Robert Leamnson, *Thinking about Teaching and Learning* (Stirling, VA: Stylus, 1999), 8.
26. Leamnson, *Thinking about Teaching and Learning*, 54.
27. Parker J. Palmer, "The Heart of a Teacher: Identity and Integrity in Teaching," *Change* 29, no. 6 (November/December 1997): 15.
28. *Oxford English Dictionary*, s.v. "respect."
29. Palmer, "The Heart of a Teacher: Identity and Integrity in Teaching," 18.
30. Third child (oldest son) of Hyrum Smith and Jerusha Barden. He was born September 22, 1832, making him twenty-four years old.
31. Heber C. Kimball (first counselor in the First Presidency).
32. *Oxford English Dictionary*, s.v. "wisdom."
33. Boyd K. Packer, in Conference Report, April 1997, 8.
34. Albert Jesse Smith was born September 16, 1881, and died, as stated in the letter, August 25, 1883.
35. Sixth child of Hyrum Smith and Jerusha Barden; born October 2, 1837; died November 6, 1876.

36. Oldest child of Hyrum Smith and Jersuha Barden; born September 16, 1827; died October 8, 1876.
37. Job 13:15.
38. Job 1:21.
39. Jeffrey R. Holland, in Conference Report, April 1998, 31–34.

Christ with St. Joseph in the Carpenter's Shop, by Georges de La Tour (1593-1652). The Louvre, Paris.

Christmas and Childhood

J. R. Kearl

J. R. Kearl *is the Abraham O. Smoot Professor of Economics at BYU and assistant to the president for the Jerusalem Center for Near Eastern Studies.*

Each year, members of The Church of Jesus Christ of Latter-day Saints join much of the Christian world in celebrating Christmas. And each year, the approaching holiday season causes me to think about the contrast between Christmas and Easter—the other great celebration of Christ's life. I invite everyone to join me in reflecting on the distinctive spirit of the Christmas season and its associated celebration of Jesus's birth. In particular, I invite good people everywhere to think about the words and associated memories that come to mind when we think of the word *Christmas*. For me, words like *expectation, anticipation, hope, potential, awe, wonder, spontaneity, joy,* and *curiosity* capture some of the feel of Christmas.

Now think for a moment about the word *Easter*. Are your thoughts the same as when you reflect on the meaning of *Christmas,* or do you see in your imagination and feel in your hearts something slightly different? I do. When I think of *Easter*, words like *fulfillment, realization,* and *triumph* seem to best capture my feelings.

For me, the difference between Christmas and Easter parallels the music we commonly sing at Christmastime: "Silent Night," "With Wondering Awe," "O Little Town of Bethlehem," or "Away in a Manger." These traditional Christmas hymns have a softness and tenderness that whispers, "Shush—there's a babe over there lying in a manger." By contrast, when I think of moving or inspirational Easter hymns, I think of "He Is Risen," "Christ the Lord

Is Risen Today," or similar majestic anthems that in their voicing proclaim, "Christ is triumphant!"

This difference between the quiet potential of Christmas and the acknowledged realization of Easter is also manifest in scriptural records. Consider, for example, the account of angels announcing the Messiah's birth to a few shepherds in the hills near Bethlehem. While these same angels joined heavenly hosts in singing "Glory to God," they apparently did so to only a handful of earthly observers, as we find no scriptural evidence of a widespread understanding that Jesus Christ, the Son of God, had just come to earth as a mortal infant.

By contrast, at the beginning of the last week of His life, Jesus rode triumphantly into Jerusalem on a donkey, through streets mobbed by people spreading a carpet of palm fronds at His feet. While virtually all would abandon Him by the end of the week and demand His crucifixion when offered the choice between freeing Him or Barabbas, at the beginning of the week, there could not have been many people in Jerusalem or in the surrounding area who did not know that Jesus had arrived in the city.

For me, the difference between Christmas and Easter is also illuminated by a stunningly beautiful painting I first saw in the Louvre nearly twenty years ago. I was wandering around at the end of a long morning, a bit numb and almost overcome by a museum as large and rich in visual delights as the Louvre. As I turned a corner, I saw the painting by Georges de La Tour. It is entitled simply *Christ with St. Joseph in the Carpenter's Shop*.

From the first moment I saw this painting, I was completely enthralled by its beauty and peace. Obviously, thousands—perhaps tens of thousands—of nativity paintings and other images depict Jesus as an infant, typically with His mother Mary. Probably an equal number are devoted to His ministry, His suffering in Gethsemane and on the cross, and His subsequent Resurrection and ascension into heaven.

But the de La Tour painting is one of only a handful of works of Jesus as a boy. It has become my favorite painting. If I am in Paris, I make something of a pilgrimage to the Louvre to be inspired and calmed by it. I am so taken by it that a couple of years ago when my three eldest children were returning from study at the Brigham Young University Jerusalem Center, I agreed to pay for a hotel in Paris for a couple of nights on the condition they find this painting in the Louvre.

De La Tour portrays the youthful Jesus looking at His stepfather with deep affection as Jesus holds a candle to light the work of the man who was known in His community and, for much of Jesus's life, as His father. The painting conveys a sense of love, deep affection, peace, innocence, and purity—each a wonderful attribute of Christmas and of childhood. For me, de La Tour has captured much of what Christmas represents. He does so through the eyes of a young boy, an innocent young boy. Don't all of us, in a way, see Christmas through the eyes of children?

Given that we most often see Christmas in this light, I am surprised at how little attention is actually paid to Jesus's childhood. It is not just art that ignores His childhood and focuses primarily on His birth, later ministry, atoning sacrifice, and Resurrection. The scriptural story of Jesus's earthly sojourn is also mostly silent from the flight into Egypt at around the age of two until He begins His ministry by journeying to be baptized by John in the Jordan River as a mature man, perhaps thirty years old. The notable exception is the scriptural appearance of Christ at about age twelve when the group He and His family had joined to journey from Nazareth to Jerusalem left Jerusalem for the long journey back to Nazareth without Him. Listen to the voice of Mary, who is clearly, in this instance, not the mother of Jesus the Son of God but the mother of Jesus the child, almost a teenager:

> And when he was twelve years old, they went up to Jerusalem after the custom of the feast.
>
> And when they had fulfilled the days, as they returned, the child Jesus tarried behind in Jerusalem; and Joseph and his mother knew not of it.
>
> But they, supposing him to have been in the company, went a day's journey; and they sought him among their kinsfolk and acquaintance.
>
> And when they found him not, they turned back to Jerusalem, seeking him.
>
> And it came to pass, that after three days they found him in the temple. . . .
>
> And his mother said unto him, Son, why hast thou thus dealt with us?
>
> Behold, thy father and I have sought thee sorrowing. . . .

And he went down with them, and came to Nazareth,
and was subject unto them. (Luke 2:42–51)

How many of us have heard that voice in our own mothers' expressions of concern about our being out a bit too late on a date or driving on snow-packed and icy winter roads?

Beyond this single account, we know virtually nothing else about Jesus's life between the ages of two and thirty. Isaiah does tell us that Jesus's childhood and young adulthood would not be easy: "Therefore the Lord himself shall give you a sign; Behold, a virgin shall conceive, and bear a son, and shall call his name Immanuel. Butter and honey shall he eat, that he may know to refuse the evil and choose the good" (Isaiah 7:14–16). "For he shall grow up before him as a tender plant, and as a root out of dry ground" (Isaiah 53:2).

"Butter," probably better translated as "curd," is not meant in this scripture to imply wealth or luxury but just the opposite: the harsh and difficult conditions of the poor at the time. Archaeological and other evidence suggest that life at the time was probably short—not more than forty years if a person survived early childhood. Evidence also suggests that nutrition was inadequate. However, Isaiah suggests that growing up in Jesus's particular environment was important in forming the person who subsequently chose to take upon Himself our sins.

The Son of a Carpenter, by François Lafon.
Church of St. Joseph, Nazareth, Israel.

We know that Jesus grew up in a very small village of perhaps two hundred people, most of whom were probably part of His extended family. He was known as the son of a carpenter: "Is not this the carpenter's son?" (Matthew 13:55) and as Joseph and Mary's son. Mark tells us that Jesus was Himself a carpenter: "Is this not the carpenter?" (Mark 6:3).

Imagine Jesus as an apprentice in Joseph's workshop. The painting that comes to my mind at this point, one more of a few of Jesus as a child or young adult, is from St. Joseph's Church, built over the traditional site of Joseph's shop in Nazareth. While not as powerful as the de La Tour painting, it does convey the notion of apprenticeship and of parents gathered around and working with a maturing boy. Even in the de la Tour painting, Jesus is at work with Joseph. De La Tour has Joseph bending over with a primitive brace and bit, drilling on the dimly lit beam at his feet while Jesus shields the candle flame from any breeze as He lights his stepfather's work.

We also know from the scriptural record that Jesus grew up in a fairly large family. Both Mark and Matthew tell us of four brothers—James, Joses, Juda, and Simon—and unnamed sisters (Mark 6:3; Matthew 13:55–56).

Finally, we can infer from the scriptural record that Jesus had affection for Nazareth, the village where He grew up. We can see this in a kind of backhanded way when, in the excitement that many of us understand about returning as an adult to our childhood home, He is disappointed and clearly very pained by His reception in Nazareth. Listen to His voice on this occasion: "And he went out from thence, and came into his own country. . . . And when the sabbath day was come, he began to teach in the synagogue: and many hearing him were astonished, saying, From whence hath this man these things? and what wisdom is this which is given unto him, that even such mighty works are wrought by his hands? . . . And they were offended at him. But Jesus said unto them, A prophet is not without honour, but in his own country, and among his own kin, and in his own house" (Mark 6:1–4).

Significantly, *we know almost nothing* about the period between Jesus's birth and the beginning of His ministry thirty years later. The absence of a scriptural record is, I believe, neither an accident nor an oversight. While working through divine inspiration, Joseph Smith expanded and corrected the Bible, leaving the account of Jesus's childhood untouched. This was not an oversight, as the Prophet clearly felt comfortable expanding, to a considerable degree, the scriptural account of Melchizedek's life. The difference between his treatment of Melchizedek's life and Jesus's early life suggests that

God, Jesus's mortal father, clearly wanted His Only Begotten Son to grow up in the kind of environment typical for children and young adults of the time—protected and sheltered from the adult world He would enter, but only as an adult.

Think about it for a moment. Jesus Christ, the literal Son of God, virtually disappears from the scriptural record from the age of two to the age of thirty. What does He disappear into? He disappears into childhood, into teenage years, and into young adulthood in a small village in the hills near the Sea of Galilee, there to grow up among brothers, sisters, cousins, aunts, uncles, neighbors, and friends.

I believe that this *disappearance* of Jesus into childhood wasn't by chance but happened by heavenly design. There is something so important that occurs during these formative years that our Father in Heaven wanted His Son to experience it. In other words, it was important for Jesus to be not only the Son of God but also the child of Mary and Joseph and the brother of James with other brothers and sisters around Him. Something very significant about childhood warranted this extraordinary occurrence in which the Son of God literally disappeared into childhood and did not reappear until He was an adult.

In Conan Doyle's *Silver Blaze*, Watson asks Holmes, "Is there any point to which you would wish to draw my attention?"

Holmes replies, "To the curious incident of the dog in the night-time."

Watson observes, "The dog did nothing in the night-time."

Holmes responds, "That was the curious incident."[1]

For Holmes, silence was a clue. Similarly, the silent scriptural record is, I believe, a clue to at least two things about Jesus's life from age two to age thirty. First, Jesus had a *protected* childhood. Indeed, it remains protected in precisely the sense that we know virtually nothing about it and are clearly not supposed to. Second, Jesus had an *extended* childhood. If ever there was a child who could have matured quickly and assumed His divinely appointed role and mission, it is Jesus Christ, the literal Son of God. Yet, with what must be seen as great patience, His earthly father and Heavenly Father allowed Jesus to mature slowly—in short, to have a childhood.

We live, unfortunately, in a world that intrudes on childhood and that wants to deprive it of innocence, charm, faith, trust, hope, and even peace and security—all the things that make childhood rich and important. We live in a world that literally wants to rob children of childhood. In doing so, the world robs them of the joy that maybe comes to children only when they are able to live protected to some degree from the world with innocence, faith, trust, and security.

Kiku Adatto, director of the Children's Studies Program at Harvard, noted: "We're obsessed with children, but that doesn't mean the same thing as upholding the idea of childhood. In fact, we're obsessed with it [children] precisely because all the barriers between childhood and adulthood are breaking down."[2] As an example of this breakdown, Adatto's group at Harvard studied photos of children taken throughout this century and found that children's pictures that once paid homage to childhood innocence have increasingly given way to sexualized images of ever-younger childlike models in ads for cologne, underwear, jeans, or the like.[3]

Stephanie Coontz, author of *The Way We Really Are*, notes that for years, children were excluded from adult knowledge and participation in the adult world. "Now," she says, "we try to exclude them from participation, but we're unable to exclude them from knowledge. It's the most pathological situation [imaginable]."[4]

Kay S. Hymowitz, who wrote "Tweens: Ten Going on Sixteen," suggests that absentee parents—due primarily to parents working long hours away from home—and a "sexualized and glitzy media-driven marketplace" have pushed young children into settings where peer expectations encourage choices regarding dress, language, and behavior that were once confronted by young people five, six, or even ten years later.[5]

There is legitimate concern and much hand-wringing these days about a world that intrudes with adult themes and issues in our homes and in our children's lives. I'm hardly the first to point to what appears to be an unrelenting assault on childhood. It is important that, as prophets have counseled, we fortify our homes against these intrusions—that we protect our children's childhoods. There is much that we can and ought to do in this effort. Though it goes beyond the purpose of this essay to do more than encourage all of us in this effort, it is worth taking note of Isaiah's counsel: "And all thy children shall be taught of the Lord; and great shall be the peace of thy children" (Isaiah 54:13).

That is a remarkable promise. If we teach our children of—that is, about—the Lord and teach them to love the scriptures and the words of prophets that testify and teach of Him, our children *will have peace*. Note that the promised reward of "peace" is for our children *as children*, not as adults, and not for us as parents, at least directly. Note also that the scripture can be read to suggest that our children will, if we create the environment, be taught by the Lord.

However, we make a mistake if we believe that it is we against the world in protecting childhood. Indeed, I want to suggest that we are often coconspirators with the world in robbing our children of their childhoods. "How so?" you might ask. My answer is that we are coconspirators because we relentlessly push our children to grow up too fast.

As noted earlier, it was not simply that Jesus had a protected childhood; He also had an *extended* childhood. We are aware of a world that would intrude on childhood. Are we equally aware of our own efforts to shorten childhood? Think of the stereotypical example: Little League—a game in which boys dress like men and are pushed to perform like men while their fathers stand on the sidelines and act childish. Don't we too often give extraordinary attention to children who seem particularly precocious—that is, to those who seem particularly adult?

There is a pride, a false pride, in boasting about our children being the "youngest" to have accomplished such and such (typically adult) feats. Thus, while we bemoan the encroachment of the world into our homes, complaining that an intrusive adult world forces our children to confront adult themes and adult issues before we think they ought to, at exactly the same time, we push our children out of childhood and out of important teenage experiences. In short, we push them to act like adults, to take on adult activities, and to perform like adults well before they *are* adults. In doing so, we rob our children of their precious childhoods just as surely as does a world that seems hostile to childhood.

Here is an example of what I'm saying. A few years ago, I held an administrative position at Brigham Young University where I dealt with appeals from parents on admissions matters. Among the most difficult for me were appeals from parents whose children had been denied "early admission"—that is, from those parents who believed that the proper place for their children who were fourteen, fifteen, or sixteen years old was with young adults in a university setting. The common complaint was, "There's nothing left for them to do in high school." On occasion, I responded, "Well, except to attend the junior prom."

This answer, meant to be semiserious but not flippant, always drew an icy silence from the other end of the telephone line. I note, parenthetically, that I have five children. Over the past decade or so, I have had five fifteen-year-old teenagers living in my home. So I can understand the natural urge of parents, on occasion, wanting to have their teenagers somewhere else or, perhaps, *anywhere* else. But it's precisely because I sometimes wanted my children somewhere else that I came to understand the realities of such thinking. Maturing takes time—even apparently for the Son of God, and the development of the attributes that really matter requires both a protected and an extended childhood.

With regard to this urge to push our children through schooling as rapidly as possible, what is it about the world of adult work that makes us so anxious to push our children into it? Do we really believe that entering the world of full-time work or embarking on a career as soon as possible results in a better life than learning about and enjoying teenage years and then entering the workforce and beginning a career in a timely fashion after high school, college, or technical training is completed?

Curiously, adults often look back with nostalgia at precisely the teenage years in their own lives and yet seem so eager to push their children quickly through this time period. Michael and Diane Medved frame this situation nicely when they suggest that a protected and extended childhood allows children the luxury to concentrate on really important things while, by contrast, adults are forced to give attention to those things that are merely urgent.[6]

The murder several years ago of seven-year-old Jon Benet Ramsey was shocking. It was shocking because no child ought to be deprived of life in that manner and at that age. But wasn't it also shocking to see a child dressed up to effect the look of a twenty-year-old woman? Whatever one thinks of beauty pageants or contests for twenty-year-old young women, there is something deeply upsetting and disturbing about a seven-year-old child made to pretend that this is her world. Perhaps what stunned people about this tragic murder is that the photo was a caricature, or even a mirror, in which we saw something of our own efforts to force our children to grow up too quickly and before their time.

Surely, if ever a precocious child has lived on the earth, that child is Jesus Christ, the literal Son of God. Yet our Father in Heaven apparently wanted His Son to mature slowly—to enjoy childhood, teenage years, and even young adulthood, protected from an untimely entrance into the adult world. We have no evidence that He was pushed to become something before

He was an adult, although surely Jesus could have been anything He wanted to be at almost any time during those years. Abundant evidence exists to show that He was protected. In fact, the lack of a scriptural record speaks eloquently, in its silence, to this fact.

Where the scriptural record does speak, it clearly suggests that He *grew* up. Luke records that after Jesus's birth, the family "returned into Galilee, to their own city Nazareth. And the child grew, and waxed strong in spirit, filled with wisdom: and the grace of God was upon him" (Luke 2:39–40). Then, after the journey to Jerusalem in which Jesus was left behind and after His frantic parents searched for three days, we read that He "came to Nazareth, and was subject unto them. . . . And Jesus increased in wisdom and stature, and in favour with God and man" (Luke 2:51–52). Note that Luke's first observation is about the period between Jesus's birth and His appearance in the temple at about the age of twelve and that the second refers to the period after His visit to the temple—that is, the period when He would have been a teenager.

Paul observed, "Though he were a Son, yet learned he obedience by the things which he suffered"—that is, experienced (Hebrews 5:8). And from a modern text written by John and revealed to the Prophet Joseph Smith, we learn: "And I, John, saw that he received not of the fulness at the first, but received grace for grace . . . [and] continued from grace to grace, until he received a fulness; And thus he was called the Son of God" (D&C 93:12).

Joseph Smith's inspired translation of the Bible provides some additional insight: "And it came to pass that Jesus grew up with his brethren, and waxed strong, and waited upon the Lord for the time of his ministry to come. And he served under his father, and he spake not as other men, neither could he be taught; for he needed not that any man should teach him. And after many years, the hour of his ministry drew nigh" (JST, Matthew 3:24–26).

The clear sense of these passages is that Jesus grew up by passing through a childhood and youth that were the norm for His day.

In regard to our own children's growing up, Neil Postman, author of *The Disappearance of Childhood*, argues that an "adult knows about certain facets of life—its mysteries, its contradictions, its violence, its tragedies—that are not considered suitable for children to know. . . . As children move toward adulthood, we reveal these things to them."[7] But we do so slowly and in a timely fashion. In this regard, Mitchell Kalpakgian argues that for children to become intellectually complete adults, they need "a true childhood [that] provides leisure and light-mindedness—an atmosphere of play that stimulates the creative imagination and nourishes the inner life of the mind and soul."[8]

I don't want to be misunderstood. We protect childhood not by nostalgic indulgence but by a recognition that while childhood exhibits attributes that are extraordinarily important and wonderful, children are also born impulsive, self-centered, and irresponsible. An important part of an extended childhood is helping children to learn to value and cooperate with others, to delay gratification, and to establish realistic connections between their behavior and its consequences. This maturing process requires both biological maturation and years of sustained parental effort. It is not easy to teach children to be considerate, empathetic, and moral or to behave ethically and with a generous heart and spirit. The crucial learning environment to develop these attributes is one that combines affection, discipline, example, emotional space, and, very importantly, time. That is to say, the crucial learning environment is an extended, as well as a protected, childhood.

I also don't want to be thought to be Pollyannaish or naive or to be understood to be arguing that we should not prepare, in a timely way, our children for the world in which they will live. But I confess that I cringe a bit when I read or hear a public service ad that asks, "Have you talked with your child yet about sexually transmitted diseases?" or "Have you talked with your child yet about drugs and drug abuse?" Perhaps such discussions are necessary; but, if so, it's surely a damning indictment of our age that they are. Moreover, the argument that our children are going to have to face such and such an issue at some point anyway so they may as well face it now is specious and wrongheaded. It is an argument that invariably brings adult issues and concerns into our children's lives at earlier and earlier points. Might it not be true that precisely because our children will have to face certain specific issues at some point, they ought to be protected from those issues as children? That is, isn't it likely that an extended and protected childhood best equips them for the world they will have to confront as adults?

The Christmas season is a wonderful season—one that gives us the opportunity to see once again what a beautiful and extraordinary world this is when seen through the eyes of children. Christmas not only is "for children" but also is a holiday in celebration of childhood. Christmas is in its transcendent meaning also a celebration of Jesus's mission of redemption. The child who holds the candle to light the work of the father Jesus knew in Nazareth, as reflected in the de La Tour painting, becomes literally the light of the world when He enters it as an adult, fully prepared by His heavenly heritage and by a protected and extended childhood in the hills of Nazareth.

Although redemption is the central, glorious, and sublime message of Christmas, in its particulars—that is, its language—and in the memories and images that Christmas evokes, Christmas is also a celebration of childhood. I hope that at each Christmas season we may reflect on this fact and pause to think not just about how we might protect our children's childhoods from an intrusive world but also about how we can protect our children's childhoods from our own inclinations to push them to become something too soon.

This wonderful season gives us the opportunity to see, once again, what a beautiful and extraordinary world we live in when it is seen through the eyes of children. I pray that, whatever our age, we might seek to see it in this way, at any time of the year, and that we might rejoice in those attributes that make children, as children, so special.

Notes

1. Arthur Conan Doyle, "Silver Blaze," *Sherlock Holmes' Greatest Cases* (New York: Franklin Watts, 1967), 423.
2. Peter Applebome, "No Room for Children in a World of Little Adults," *New York Times*, May 10, 1998, 9.
3. Applebome, "No Room for Children," 10.
4. Applebome, "No Room for Children," 10.
5. Kay S. Hymowitz, "Kids Today Are Growing Up Way Too Fast," *Wall Street Journal*, October 28, 1998, A22.
6. Michael Medved and Diane Medved, *Saving Childhood* (New York: HarperCollins, 1998).
7. Neil Postman, *The Disappearance of Childhood* (New York: Vintage, 1994), 15.
8. Mitchell Kalpakgian, "Why the Entertainment Industry Is Bad for Children," *New Oxford Review* 63, no. 2 (March 1996): 14.

"Those Who See": A Century's Charge to Religious Educators

Scott C. Esplin and Brent R. Esplin

Scott C. Esplin *is an assistant professor of Church history and doctrine at BYU.* **Brent R. Esplin** *is institute director at the Cedar City Institute of Religion at Southern Utah University.*

A couple of years ago I taught "that class"—thirty-five freshmen, twenty-seven of them boys.[1]

I'm sure every teacher has had or eventually will have a class like that. Maybe everyone needs one. Naturally, it was fifth period, right after lunch (it seems like it always is). By winter, the idealism of a new year the Church Educational System (CES) symposium had worn off, and I was frustrated. I was most bothered by a statement made by President J. Reuben Clark Jr. in "The Charted Course of the Church in Education." He promised teachers: "The youth of the Church are hungry for things of the spirit; they are eager to learn the gospel, and they want it straight, undiluted. They want to know. . . . These students crave the faith. . . . They are prepared to understand the truth."[2]

My students were hungry all right—but not for anything I was offering. Obviously, he had not seen my class.

That year I had on my wall a quote taken from President Boyd K. Packer's talk to religious educators in which he quoted President Joseph F. Smith, who said: "The hand of the Lord may not be visible to all. There may be many who cannot discern the workings of God's will in the progress and development of this great latter-day work, *but there are those who see in every hour and in every moment of the existence of the Church, from its beginning until now, the overruling, almighty hand of Him who sent His Only Begotten Son.*"[3]

In the winter of that year, I was far from seeing the hand of the Lord "in every hour and in every moment" of my class. I began to wonder if He spent "any hour" or "any moment" in my class and whether I could handle others like it for the next forty years.

But President Smith testified, "There are those who see." Who are they, and what do they see? What is the prophetic vision of religious education? President Packer, speaking of CES employees, observed: "I would like to make just a comment or two about the assignments that are mine as one of the General Authorities. . . . I have learned firsthand how the General Authorities of the Church regard this group. I now know the importance of this body of men, and I do not know whether it is quite what I expected it to be. It is a good deal finer that I hoped it would be. And I know now, firsthand, how tremendously important this body is in reference to the destiny of the Church."[4]

On another occasion, President Packer again noted: "In the history of the Church there is no better illustration of the prophetic preparation of this people than the beginnings of the seminary and institute program. These programs were started when they were nice but were not critically needed. They were granted a season to flourish and to grow into a bulwark for the Church. They now become a godsend for the salvation of modern Israel in a most challenging hour. We are now encircled. Our youth are in desperate jeopardy. These are the last days, foreseen by prophets in ancient times."[5]

Prophets do not use phrases like "tremendously important," "prophetic preparation," and "godsend" lightly. As they are blessed with spiritual insight into youth and education, what do they see? How do prophets feel about religious education? Why do they feel so strongly?

These questions sparked our search of talks by General Authorities relative to education. Since 1938, nearly 150 talks by General Authorities have been directed to the CES audience. Addresses include messages delivered at BYU summer school conventions, CES symposia (conferences), annual "Evening with a General Authority" gatherings, and CES satellite training broadcasts. These talks, covering seventy years, represent what President Packer called "the prophetic preparation"[6] of the CES as well as the combined educational vision of over forty of the Lord's anointed.

The Law of Teaching

The talks of the century reveal a pattern that conforms to the directives the Lord has given for teaching. In 1987, President Ezra Taft Benson questioned, "Are we using the messages and method of teaching found in the Book of Mormon and other scriptures of the Restoration to teach this great plan of the Eternal God?"[7]

What did he mean by "the method of teaching found in the [scriptures]"? Is there a method of teaching the Lord has given us and expects us to use in teaching His gospel? If so, where is it found? If there is a method, do General Authorities teach and model it when they train?

The Lord outlined elements of a teaching model in the section Joseph Smith referred to as "the law of the Church." The Doctrine and Covenants describes a "law of teaching" in the following words: "And again, the elders, priests, and teachers of this church shall teach the principles of my gospel, which are in the Bible and the Book of Mormon, in the which is the fulness of the gospel. And they shall observe the covenants and church articles to do them, and these shall be their teachings, as they are directed by the Spirit" (D&C 42:12–13).

The Lord's law of teaching includes four elements: teaching principles and doctrines, observing covenants, obeying Church articles, and being directed by the Spirit. The talks to religious educators discuss and model each of these four elements.

"The Charted Course":
A Beginning Place for Finding the Lord's Method

The first published address, "The Charted Course of the Church in Education," holds a special place in establishing religious education. Since the talk's delivery, prophets have continually referred to it, holding it up as a model. Of President Clark's landmark talk, President Henry B. Eyring said: "The place I would always begin, to be sure I knew what those principles are, would be to read President J. Reuben Clark Jr.'s talk 'The Charted Course of the Church in Education.' . . . He saw our time and beyond, with prophetic insight. The principles he taught, of how to see our students and thus how to teach them, will always apply in our classrooms. . . . The great change in our classrooms, as the kingdom goes forth to every nation, kindred, tongue, and people, will only verify the prophetic vision of President Clark. . . . The principles described so many years ago will be a sure guide in the years ahead."[8]

President Packer wrote of the same address: "President Clark was a prophet, seer, and revelator. There is not the slightest question but that exceptional inspiration attended the preparation of his message. There is a clarity and power in his words, unusual even for him. . . . Read it carefully and ponder it. For by applying the definition the Lord Himself gave, this instruction may comfortably be referred to as scripture."[9]

Prophets feel so strongly about the principles outlined in "The Charted Course" that they quote liberally from it. In his 1980 address to religious educators, President Marion G. Romney scrapped a previously prepared speech (as indicated by President Eyring[10]), declaring instead, "Because this assignment to speak to you professional teachers about how to teach the gospel of Jesus Christ in these Church institutions requires an endowment which I do not possess, I shall say what I think should be said in the words of President J. Reuben Clark, Jr."[11] He then proceeded to quote word for word from "The Charted Course of the Church in Education."

President Eyring later spoke of that night and the car ride with President Romney following the talk. He questioned: "'President Romney, don't you think young people and the world have changed almost completely since President Clark gave that talk in 1938? . . . Do you think what President Clark taught still describes the way we should approach our students today?' President Romney chuckled, sat silent for a moment, and then said, 'Oh, I think President Clark could see our time and beyond.'"[12]

President Clark's vision of "our time and beyond" includes, like Doctrine and Covenants 42:12–13, a discussion of doctrine, covenants, articles (teaching counsel), and Spirit-directed teaching. Interestingly, it does not include any mention of the conditions of the day, although the talk was given at the beginning of World War II in Europe and the end of the Great Depression. His words are not time-sensitive, with statements such as "in our troubled times," "in light of what is taking place," or "with this on the horizon." Like scripture, the talk transcends time and circumstance, stating facts as if they were applicable to any time or place in history. As stated by President Romney, a fellow member of the First Presidency, President Clark possessed "an endowment" unique to the situation.[13]

In the rest of this article, we will analyze the four elements of the Lord's teaching method outlined in Doctrine and Covenants 42:12–13. The sections will include President Clark's words on the subject, supported by prophetic commentary from fellow General Authorities in their counsel to CES employees. Finally, it will include a summary of how the Brethren feel about students, teachers, and the role of religious education in the destiny of the Church.

Doctrine

Doctrine, as used in Doctrine and Covenants 42:12, refers to the "principles of [the] gospel, which are in the Bible and the Book of Mormon." From President Clark's time until today, doctrine has received a strong emphasis in the talks to CES by General Authorities, with over sixty talks dealing with the subject. Elder Mark E. Petersen declared: "Our *authorities are the scriptures, the four standard works.* Joseph Smith and the *other Presidents and leaders are likewise our authorities.* They are our file leaders. We must teach as they do. We must *avoid the doctrines which they avoid,* we must avoid the practices which they avoid.[14]

President Clark likewise stated:

> There is neither reason nor is there excuse for our Church religious teaching and training facilities and institutions, unless the youth are to be taught and trained in the principles of the Gospel, embracing therein the two great elements that Jesus is the Christ and that Joseph was God's prophet. The teaching of a system of ethics to the students is not a sufficient reason for running our seminaries and institutes. . . . There are the great principles involved in eternal life, the Priesthood, the resurrection, and many like other things that go way beyond these canons of good living. These great fundamental principles also must be taught to the youth; they are *the things the youth wish first to know about.*[15]

He continued:

> You do have an interest in matters purely cultural and in matters of purely secular knowledge; but, I repeat again for emphasis, *your chief interest, your essential and all but sole duty, is to teach the Gospel* of the Lord Jesus Christ as that has been revealed in these latter days. You are to teach this Gospel *using as your sources and authorities the Standard Works of the Church, and the words of those whom God has called* to lead His people in these last days. You are *not, whether high or low, to intrude into your work your own peculiar philosophy,* no matter what its

source or how pleasing or rational it seems to you to be. . . . You are *not, whether high or low, to change the doctrines* of the Church or to modify them.[16]

The Power of Doctrine

Prophets give promises for the power of doctrine in teaching. Elder Bruce R. McConkie testified: "You do not change anybody's life by teaching them mathematics. . . . But you do change the lives of people when you teach them the doctrines of salvation."[17]

Elder Jeffrey R. Holland declared: "The Church has a great work to do, and we want to do it right down the middle of the straight and narrow path. Teach the gospel. Teach the doctrine. It has all the power and appeal you will ever need to hold your students."[18]

The Doctrines to Teach

With faith that the teaching of doctrine has power, what constitutes "doctrine" in the CES classroom? Speaking of the Brethren, Elder Petersen noted, "We must avoid the doctrines which they avoid."[19]

What doctrines do the Brethren teach? What do they avoid? Have they modeled them for the CES? President Harold B. Lee counseled teachers: "You as teachers are not being sent out to teach new doctrines. You're to teach the old doctrines, not so plainly that they can just understand, but *you must teach the doctrines of the Church so plainly that no one can misunderstand.*"[20]

Part of the "plain teaching" includes teaching to the proper audience. Just because something may be true does not mean it needs to be taught in the classroom. President Packer warned: "There is a temptation for the writer or the teacher . . . to want to tell everything, whether it is worthy or faith promoting or not. Some things that are true are not very useful. . . . The writer or the teacher who has an exaggerated loyalty to the theory that everything must be told is laying a foundation for his own judgment. . . . It matters very much not only *what* we are told but *when* we are told it. Be careful that you build faith rather than destroy it."[21]

Because of this warning, the Brethren have provided powerful aids to help a teacher determine the appropriateness of doctrine. One aid is the document "Basic Doctrine," published in the *Charge to Religious Educators*, third edition. The two-page document lists and develops "basic doctrines and general objectives . . . approved by the Church Board of Education."[22]

General Authorities' talks are another aid. Again, as Elder Petersen stated, "We must avoid the doctrines which they avoid."[23]

Teachers can look to the prophets as a model for doctrinal teaching, as almost half of the talks deal with doctrine. Most come from an era of doctrinal discussion, the 1950s and 1960s, when authorities like Joseph Fielding Smith and Harold B. Lee established the doctrine and modeled its teaching.

A third, and probably the greatest, aid in teaching true doctrine has been provided by the Lord Himself. Elder McConkie taught: "The scriptures themselves present the gospel in the way that the Lord wants it presented to us in our day.... We are to teach in the way things are recorded in the standard works that we have. And if you want to know what emphasis should be given to gospel principles, you simply teach the whole standard works and, automatically, in the process, you will have given the Lord's emphasis to every doctrine and every principle."[24]

Warnings about Teaching the Sensational

When explaining doctrine, instructors are warned against teaching the sensational. President Spencer W. Kimball cautioned:

> There may be a tendency, perhaps there may be a temptation, for some institute and seminary teachers to want to delve deeply into things which we are not primarily concerned with in the eternal life of our youth. Perhaps they do this to get something that would be somewhat spectacular; something that is not known; something a little strange; a little different; or something that hadn't been dug out.... A teacher is doing a disservice to his students when he incites curiosity or encourages discussion about those things which are not a part of their lives or of their experiences.... The teachers should confine themselves to the practical standard living phases and not expound spectacular, strange, and exciting newnesses.[25]

President James E. Faust observed: "I have wondered if a few gospel scholars, including Church educators, get bored with everyday life, with the basics, and with the first principles and fundamentals of the gospel. Some seem to find the esoteric intriguing. These miracles and mysteries hold some fascination. All of us would do well to teach principles and covenants that build faith more than to teach history and geography."[26]

Elder Holland summarized the challenge with this warning:

> For the sake of the Church and your students and the gospel we love and teach, brethren and sisters, please work hard at staying balanced and steady, not given to extremism or rumors, sensationalism or fads of various kinds that often sweep through the land (and sometimes come among the members of the Church). In this regard you can be for us, and we hope with us, part of a solution, and never part of a problem.
>
> I know the challenge of trying to hold a class's attention. Every teacher wants to be a pied piper, in the very best sense, appealing to a student for the right reasons and mesmerizing them with our grasp of gospel truths. In this audience you and I know how demanding that is hour after hour, day after day, week after week. Teaching effectively, teaching powerfully, teaching with enthusiasm, solid preparation, and appealing supporting materials, that's hard work—it's among the hardest work I know and surely among the hardest work I have ever done. But please resist the temptation to push into the sensational or the extreme any doctrine you teach or any counsel you may give.[27]

We are, therefore, to teach the basic doctrines of the Church as found in the standard works and the words of the prophets. These are, after all, "the things the youth wish first to know about," according to President Clark. In concluding his address, he summarized: "The tithing represents too much toil, too much self-denial, too much sacrifice, too much faith, to be used for the colorless instruction of the youth of the Church in elementary ethics. . . . In saying this, I am speaking for the First Presidency."[28]

Covenants

Prophets have stressed that there is more to teaching than merely declaring true doctrine. President Eyring added a second aspect when he stated, "If we make the doctrine simple and clear, and if we teach out of our own changed hearts, the change for them [the students] will come."[29]

Elder Neal A. Maxwell likewise reminisced on his own seminary experience: "My own memories of my teachers at Granite High Seminary . . . are basically now distilled into what they *were* in terms of their character. Forgotten are the specific lesson menus, but I remember the chefs! It's likely to be that way with you. You will be remembered not only for what you taught, but even more for what you are."[30]

President Romney emphasized the power of a teacher's example: "I would prefer that he [the teacher] were a little off on whether the pearly gates swing in or out than not to be living so he can go through them."[31]

In another address, he observed, "I never pay any attention to a person's interpretations of the gospel if I know he isn't keeping the commandments."[32]

The Lord's law of teaching in section 42 continues: "And they shall observe the covenants." Observing the covenants, from a teacher's perspective, includes commitments both in righteous living as individuals and in obligations as employees of the Church. It deals with being worthy of the Spirit, faithful to the teaching appointment, and obedient to the directions given by the scriptures, file leaders, and the Lord's servants.

What did President Clark establish in "The Charted Course" as the standard for all teachers? "The first requisite of a teacher for teaching these principles is a personal testimony of their truth. . . . No teacher who does not have a real testimony of the truth of the Gospel . . . has any place in the Church school system. If there be any such . . . he should at once resign."[33]

President Clark stressed not only the importance of possessing a testimony but also the moral and intellectual courage to declare it.

What have the Brethren taught dealing with the aspect of covenant keeping in the Lord's method of teaching? The greatest emphasis on covenant keeping seemed to be in the decade of the 1970s when covenant keeping and personal worthiness came under attack. Focusing on this time period, what did the Lord's anointed say to teachers about covenantal worthiness?

President Packer counseled teachers to "make sure that you are committed, that you are nonneutral, that you are biased, that you are one-sided, that you are on the Lord's side."[34]

He continued: "Somewhere on earth in our day our youth must, positively must, be able to tie to someone who is not confused and who is secure in his faith. . . . Somebody has to stand, face the storm, declare the truth, and let the winds blow, and be serene and composed and steady in the doing of it. That is your responsibility and your obligation as teachers."[35]

During this same time period, President Kimball declared:

> I hope that you will be such a solid rock that they can receive from you strength that can be a real deterrent to troubles.
> . . . Your students do not deserve to suffer by reason of your

problems. . . . Your students are entitled to expect years of firm spirituality in your effective teaching. . . . In a large measure, quite a large measure, young people are going to the temple for their marriages because of you. . . . They go to the temple because you went to the temple, because you have been talking about the temple. You've been telling them the joys of temple life, and so largely because of your influence, they will go to the temple after they have filled their missions.[36]

President Benson reminded teachers: "Your first responsibility as a teacher of the gospel is to prepare yourself spiritually. All of you were interviewed by a General Authority when you applied for employment in the Church Educational System. I assume most of you were asked if you possessed a testimony. . . . Your responsibility is to live as you teach. Be consistent in your life with the message you declare to your students."[37]

When we read the talks delivered over the years, it seems the Brethren have been concerned that we keep our covenants particularly in relationship to the following:

1. That we have firm testimonies of the Savior and the Prophet Joseph Smith and the courage to bear witness of them.
2. That we are true to the questions asked by the General Authorities during our interview for employment and those established in our letters of appointment.
3. That our lives are in harmony with the covenants we have personally taken.
4. That what we teach and how we live are in harmony.
5. That we are defenders of the Brethren and "teach what prophets preach."
6. That our loyalty to the doctrine and the Brethren is unequivocal.

The Lord and the Brethren stress covenant keeping on the part of the teacher because of its teaching power. Elder Maxwell summarized:

Each of you realizes, long since, that you teach what you are. It is that lesson in the memories of your students which will outlast all other lessons that you will teach. You, as a person, can bulk large in the memory of your students. Your teaching techniques will be secondary to what you are as an individual. Your traits will be more remembered, compositely, than a particular truth in a particular lesson. This is as it should be, for if our discipleship is serious, it will show, and it will be remembered. . . . You can't be a successful teacher in The Church of Jesus Christ of Latter-day Saints, nor can I, if things are not right in our eternal callings.[38]

Church Articles

As a teacher, it is not enough to teach pure doctrine and keep one's own covenants, as powerful as these two may be in the law of teaching. The Lord in Doctrine and Covenants 42 requires something more, stating, "And they shall observe the covenants and church articles to do them." What are the "church articles"? At the time of the writing of the Doctrine and Covenants, what are now sections 20 and 22 were called the "Articles and Covenants of the Church." Speaking of these revelations, Joseph Smith stated, "In this manner did the Lord continue to give us *instructions* from time to time, concerning the duties which now devolved upon us."[39]

Noah Webster's dictionary of 1828 gives the following as one of the definitions of *article:* "A single clause in a contract, account, *system of regulations,* treaty, or other writing; a particular separate *charge* or item, in an account, a term, condition, or *stipulation* in a contract."[40]

"Church articles," for our purposes, are the "instructions, duties, regulations, charges, and stipulations" that constitute being a teacher beyond merely keeping covenants. They are the instructions relative to teaching. It is not enough to live as Church articles instruct and teach pure doctrine. We must, as Elder Petersen noted, "teach as [prophets] do."[41]

So what have the prophets said specifically about teaching? How can teachers improve teaching? Elder Holland noted there is something beyond covenant keeping that constitutes valuable teaching:

> To a group of professional teachers surely it need not be belabored that, after we have prepared and purified ourselves to have the companionship of the spirit of the Lord, it is then required of us to develop genuine mastery in our profession, using the best educational techniques we can employ and honing our skills for as long as we are privileged to enter that classroom. We need to devote the same kind of effort toward improving our teaching abilities that a man or woman in any other profession would exert, be they physicians, or attorneys, or computer experts, or microbiologists. *In the Church Educational System it is essential but not sufficient that we be good men or women—we must also be good at what we do. We must be very*

good. Our subject matter and the lives of our students demand that we give our very best effort in our teaching.[42]

Elder Maxwell likewise observed the importance of effective teaching:

> Of course there are individuals who are keeping their covenants who lack teaching charisma. Of course there are those whose lives are in order who are not exciting as teachers. However, the Spirit blesses the efforts of all who live worthily. It endorses what they say or do. There is a witnessing authenticity which proceeds from the commandment keeper, which speaks for itself. Therefore, I prefer doctrinal accuracy and spiritual certitude (even with a little dullness) to charisma with unanchored cleverness.
>
> However, part of what may be lacking, at times, in the decent teacher is a freshening personal excitement over the gospel which could prove highly contagious. Since we can only speak the smallest part of what we feel, we should not let that "smallest part" shrink in its size.[43]

President Clark set the standard in improving teaching skills and magnifying the "smallest part": "Before trying on the newest fangled ideas in any line of thought, education, activity, or what not, experts should just stop and consider that however backward they think we are, and however backward we may actually be in some things, in other things we are far out in the lead, and therefore these new methods may be old, if not worn out, with us."[44]

He continued commenting on teaching methods: "You do not have to sneak up behind this spiritually experienced youth and whisper religion in his ears, you can come right out, face to face, and talk with him. . . . There is no need for gradual approaches, for 'bed-time' stories, for coddling, for patronizing, or for any of the other childish devices used in efforts to reach those spiritually inexperienced and all but spiritually dead."[45]

Teaching in the CES, therefore, is different from any other public or private teaching setting. What works elsewhere may "be old, if not worn out with us." Teaching is different because the students and the subject are different.

Teaching Gimmicks, Fads, and Games

Elder McConkie noted the difference in teaching in the Church Educational System versus other teaching. After quoting President Clark's statement on bedtime stories, coddling, patronizing, and childish devices, Elder McConkie stated, "I suppose that [statement] has some bearing on games and parties and entertainments and gimmicks which, really, brethren, are poor substitutes for teaching the doctrines of salvation to the students that you have."[46]

Elder Richard G. Scott likewise commented: "There is no place in your teaching for gimmicks, fads, or bribery by favors or treats. Such activities produce no lasting motivation for personal growth nor any enduring beneficial results. Simply stated, truths presented in an environment of true love and trust qualify for the confirming witness of the Holy Spirit."[47]

President Benson warned, "You were not hired to entertain students or unduly dramatize your message."[48]

So how do we find the balance between Elder Maxwell's "freshening personal excitement" and President Benson's "not hired to entertain . . . or unduly dramatize," especially on cold mornings in the middle of winter when the teacher may be more tired than the students?

President Eyring gave a key to effective CES teaching when he stated:

> Our aim is both that they will choose to return to our classroom daily and that they will endure in faith to the end of life. To draw them back would seem to require entertainment, and the longer haul would seem to demand some stiffer medicine. Those two aims seem incompatible, or at least very difficult to achieve in the same classroom. But it has become clear to me that what the student—even the very young student—wants in the short run is also the needed preparation for the long road ahead, however narrow in places and shrouded in mist it may turn out to be. What every student wants now is happiness. And what the student will want for the rest of life and for eternity is happiness.[49]

How do we teach happiness to a fourteen-year-old freshman boy? Almost twenty years earlier, President Eyring gave another key. In a talk to the CES administrators, he stated:

> There is a tremendous faith in the way they are revising the curriculum. The faith is that young people can be led into and love the scriptures. . . . My feeling is that there must be some way . . . to make them more using the scriptures and less using the other things and something in my heart tells me

that's right. . . . I have a hunch, if you just want my prediction, that four or five years from now you will see more Latter-day Saint youth in our classes pondering the scriptures, talking about them with each other, teaching each other from them, loving them, believing that they really do have the answers to the questions of their hearts. . . . It's going to take a miracle for young people to do that.[50]

More recently, Elder Holland has verified this focus on the scriptures, declaring: "It is little wonder that as times get tougher and the going gets rockier, the Brethren have focused our curriculum at every level, every level in the Church and every level in CES, on the scriptures. Please immerse yourself in them and immerse your students in them. Don't stray off into forbidden paths and get lost in mists of darkness. You know what happened to those folks! Stay with the rod of iron, which is the word of God. Use what teaching techniques you need to assist with your lesson, but keep war stories and strange doctrines and near-death experiences to a minimum. Stay in the heart of the mine where the real gold is."[51]

President Eyring himself recently summarized the change, "Where once there was a wealth of material calculated to hold the wandering interest of young people and even entertain them, the words of the scriptures are now doing the holding."[52]

The Brethren have counseled how to teach the scriptures to bring about this miracle. The CES is charged to teach the scriptures sequentially, using the Church-approved curriculum. President Benson illustrated his faith in these resources: "Always remember, there is no satisfactory substitute for the scriptures and the words of the living prophets. These should be your original sources. Read and ponder more what the Lord has said, and less about what others have written concerning what the Lord said. . . . As you stay with the fundamental doctrines and gospel principles, adhering to the standard works, the words of the Brethren, and your Church Educational System outlined courses of study, seeking the guidance of the Spirit, you should have no trouble following this counsel."[53]

President Eyring likewise promised: "We can unlock the power of the curriculum simply by acting on our faith that it is inspired of God. . . . Sticking with the content of the curriculum as well as its sequence will unlock our unique teaching gifts, not stifle them."[54]

What if the scriptures, the prophets, and the curriculum are silent on a question the youth may pose? President Eyring counseled:

> As we ask questions of our students we will surely stir questions in their minds. Sometimes they will ask us things which are new to us or for which we do not know the answers prophets have given. We do best at such moments to remember our purpose; it is to allow our students to be fed by hearing truth which is confirmed by the Holy Ghost. Where we have any doubt that we can answer with a fundamental and well-established truth of the gospel of Jesus Christ, we serve our students best by saying simply, "I do not know." . . . We can show students our faith that God answers every question for which we need an answer and our patience to go forward without answers to all the others.[55]

President Lee gave similar counsel: "Brethren, it is the wisest thing that you say, 'I don't know,' to the many questions of youth, when the Lord has not spoken. Never presume to elucidate upon a matter on which the Lord has revealed very little."[56]

How can a teacher have the courage to say "I don't know" to a student he or she loves and knows is struggling with a particular concern? President Howard W. Hunter warned:

> Let me give a word of caution to you. I am sure you recognize the potential danger of being so influential and so persuasive that your students build an allegiance to you rather than to the gospel. Now that is a wonderful problem to have to wrestle with, and we would only hope that all of you are such charismatic teachers. But there is a genuine danger here. That is why you have to invite your students into the scriptures themselves, not just give them your interpretation and presentation of them. That is why you must invite your students to feel the Spirit of the Lord, not just give them your personal reflection of that. That is why, ultimately, you must invite your students directly to Christ, not just to one who teaches his doctrines, however ably. You will not always be available to these students. You cannot hold their hands after they have left high school or college. And you do not need personal disciples.

> Our great task is to ground these students in what can go with them through life, to point them toward him who loves them and can guide them where none of us will go. Please make sure the loyalty of these students is to the scriptures and the Lord and the doctrines of the restored Church. Point them toward God the Father and his Only Begotten Son, Jesus Christ, and toward the leadership of the true Church. Make certain that when the glamour and charisma of your personality and lectures and classroom environment are gone that they are not left empty-handed to face the world. Give them the gifts that will carry them through when they have to stand alone. When you do this, the entire Church is blessed for generations to come.[57]

President Hunter's counsel is supported by similar statements from President Kimball and President Monson about not taking the role of parent or bishop in the lives of the students.[58]

So what have prophets said about proper teacher-student relationships? Should they do anything? While prophets remind CES teachers of their proper place, prophets also consistently talk about reaching out to students. This theme is a constant one throughout the century.

In 1958, Elder A. Theodore Tuttle stated: "You brethren must set the example in compassion and love. These students may be forgotten by everyone else, but *they should not be forgotten by you*. . . . How can you sleep without seeking after every student? I know it is difficult to reach every one. But we can do much better! That is what I am pleading for today."[59]

President Kimball requested: "I hope that if any of God's children are out in spiritual darkness, you will come to them with a lamp and light their way; if they are out in the cold of spiritual bleakness with its frigidity penetrating their bones, you will come to them with your coat and your cloak also; and when they need you to walk with them holding their hands a little way, you will walk miles and miles with them lifting them, strengthening them, encouraging them and inspiring them."[60]

"The Rescue" was not just a nice pioneer theme for the sesquicentennial.

The examples of counsel and directives on teaching are numerous. It is the most-often-mentioned topic of the talks delivered to the CES; it is covered in 60 percent of the talks. Elder Tuttle was right when he declared, "I think that the prophets, after all, are the greatest teachers in the Church."[61]

Spirit

As important as the Church-directed curriculum may be in the law of teaching, the Lord Himself includes a fourth and final phase—the Spirit. Elder Holland, citing Doctrine and Covenants 42:14, stated, "'The Spirit shall be given unto you by the prayer of faith; and if ye receive not the Spirit ye shall not teach.' . . . Not just that you won't teach or that you can't teach or that it will be pretty shoddy teaching. No, it is stronger than that. It is the imperative form of the verb. "'Ye *shall not* teach.' Put a *thou* in there for *ye* and you have Mt. Sinai language. This is a commandment. These are God's students, not yours."[62]

Elder Maxwell observed:

> I hope you find fresh ways to involve our youth in the personal reading of the scriptures. I guess the best analogy that comes to mind is that it's like a songbook. There are many melodies that need to be sung and heard, and my favorites and your favorites are not necessarily those that would attract or be relevant for the young. Only by some personal involvement with the scriptures can they find the song the scriptures would sing to them today to meet their needs. You cannot count on the curriculum—any curriculum—to respond to individual needs that adroitly and that precisely. They have to open the songbook and hear the music. It is there. It will speak to them; it will sing to them, but sometimes it's going to have to be in the privacy of their own scholarship. There is no way you and I can anticipate all those needs that precisely.[63]

Counsel given by the General Authorities over the years that deals with teaching by the Spirit includes both learning and preparing by the Spirit. In at least twelve talks dealing directly with this subject, the Brethren emphasize that all teaching is done by the Spirit: "Wherefore, I the Lord ask you this question—unto what were ye ordained? To *preach* my gospel by the Spirit, even the Comforter which was sent forth to *teach* the truth" (D&C 50:13–14; emphasis added). The Savior stated the same truth at the Last Supper: "But the Comforter, which is the Holy Ghost, . . . he shall teach you all things" (John 14:26).

This aspect of teaching has received increased emphasis since 1980. In the late 1970s and early 1980s, there seems to have been a shift in the Church and in the CES, with greater emphasis on being Spirit directed. Teaching shifted to sequential scripture study, manuals and material helps were reduced, lessons in priesthood meeting and Relief Society were rewritten, and greater emphasis was placed on parental teaching in the home. In other words, members, leaders, and teachers were encouraged to learn to follow the prompting of the Spirit in their lives rather than to rely on detailed written directives, manuals, and guidelines from Church headquarters.

President Eyring illustrated the shift: "You're going to see a streamlining and stripping away of non-essentials and an impatience with inefficiency.... There is a tremendous faith in the way they are revising the curriculum. The faith is that young people can be led into and love the scriptures."[64]

This change has already occurred, bringing with it a greater emphasis on the scriptures and teaching by the Spirit and less emphasis on materials. President Eyring's prediction of more youths pondering, talking about, teaching, loving, and believing the scriptures has been verified.[65]

What have the Brethren shared with us about teaching with fewer aids and more Spirit? Elder McConkie stated, "I do not care what I talk about. All I am concerned with is getting in tune with the Spirit and expressing the thoughts, in the best language and way that I can, that are implanted there by the power of the Spirit. The Lord knows what a congregation needs to hear, and he has provided a means to give that revelation to every preacher and every teacher."[66]

Elder L. Tom Perry counseled: "First and foremost, of course, is to teach with the Spirit. Teaching with inspiration means seeing and taking advantage of every special teaching moment that comes along or that can be purposely created. Teaching with the Spirit will let the students know of your love and especially God's love and concern for them.... It would be impossible to stand before a class 'on fire' with the Spirit of the Lord without having your soul's vibrations resound in the hearts of your students."[67]

Elder Richard G. Scott declared:

> The greatest impact of all is what they *feel* in your presence in the classroom and elsewhere.... It is the commitment to a life every hour of which is purposefully lived in compliance with the teachings and example of the Savior and of his servants. It is a commitment to constant striving to be

evermore spiritual, evermore devoted, evermore deserving to be the conduit through which the Spirit of the Lord may touch the hearts of those you are trusted to bring to a greater understanding of his teachings. . . . The most lasting impressions, the greatest teaching, and the most enduring effects for good will result from your ability to invite the Spirit of the Lord to touch the hearts and minds of those you teach.[68]

Elder Maxwell gave detailed instructions, including a list of do's and don'ts, for teaching with the Spirit. He stated:

Teaching does not remove responsibility from the teacher for prayerful and pondering preparation. Teaching by the Spirit is not the equivalent of going on "automatic pilot." . . . Seeking the Spirit is best done when we ask the Lord to take the lead of an already informed mind, in which things have been "studied out." Additionally, if we already care deeply about those to be taught, it is so much easier for the Lord to inspire us to give customized counsel and emphasis to those we teach. Thus we cannot be clinically detached when teaching by the Spirit.[69]

President Eyring shared the effects of teaching by the Spirit at the 1999 CES symposium:

I would more carefully invite the Holy Ghost as my companion. The students wouldn't see much of what I would do, since so much would be in private. But they would sense the change in me, as the Spirit softened my nature. They would notice it in my being a little more patient, a little more interested in them, a little less likely to argue or belittle, a little more likely to smile. They would notice not only that I seemed more happy but that they were more happy in our classroom. . . . If they decided to copy what they saw brought happiness in me, they might choose the right because it brings happiness and peace of companionship of the Holy Ghost. And then the Holy Ghost will teach them all things they should do to please God and so take happiness along with them, years after they are gone from our classrooms.[70]

Prophetic Visions of the CES

Prophets indeed have a vision of what the educational system can do with the youth of the Church. A final common theme of the seventy-year history of addresses to the CES is prophetic insight into the youth of the latter days and their teachers. Nearly every talk, from President Clark's time until today, includes some blessing and counsel for these two groups. Of the youth, Elder Maxwell said: "The rising generation, those seedling Saints who sit before you—ordinary as they may seem on a dull day—are being especially prepared for unique service in the last days of this dispensation. To a significant degree, you are entrusted with the shaping of their religious education—a very genuine compliment to you and a blessing to them."[71]

President Eyring prophesied of those "ordinary" kids and their future. "I can't promise you that fifty years from now one of those skinny kids in your class will, because of you, go somewhere for the Lord where it may be hard to go. But I can promise you this: more than one of them will in that future day love whatever you love and be loyal to what you are loyal. And that could come from just one class on one day, even a day in February. You are doing more good than you know."[72]

General Authorities have constantly stressed the blessings that gospel teachers enjoy. President Hunter remarked: "I have often thought how privileged you are, how fortunate you must feel, to be in a profession that not only *allows* you but quite literally *compels* you to be immersed in the holy scriptures every day. There are so many members of the Church who envy you that rare privilege, and on some days my brethren and I envy you as well."[73]

President Eyring expressed his appreciation for teachers:

> In my travel across the Church, whenever one of you is introduced to me as "our early-morning seminary teacher" or "our seminary teacher for our students at the something-or-other junior high school," I hear a note of gratitude and admiration that I hope you hear and remember. I hope you feel it on some dark mornings as you roll out of bed or at the end of a long day when some of those junior high school students want to linger to ask a question that is new and vital to them but which you have heard more times than you can remember. I suppose what keeps you going, even more than gratitude and

admiration, is the glimpse you get of what a difference it can make when you do what you do well.[74]

Elder Scott expressed his love: "You have set aside the allurement of what so many people in the world seek—material success—and have concentrated on the better, albeit, more difficult part. Eternal success through the application of eternal truth—oh how we love you for that. I wonder if you have the remotest idea of how important you are to building faith and testimony and sustaining it as the Church grows throughout the world."[75]

Great gospel teaching truly does matter. The CES program has been and is guided by a prophetic vision. President Packer, a witness and participant in the prophetic history of the CES, summarized:

> I mentioned the many things that have improved over the years. . . . *There are some things that haven't changed.* We still have the young man and his wife struggling to get through school and then moving out to seek their fortune. That man makes a choice that he will be a teacher—a teacher of the gospel—that he will devote his life to that. With that decision at once comes the fact that all the other things that he might have chosen are therefore set aside, and the realities of his chosen life are then to be accepted. He lives on a modest income, about the middle of the middle class economically. He struggles, he has children—ordinarily too many children by the world's standards. He has the realities of a worldwide program where he is moved here and there and everywhere. . . . Well, in spite of all of those realities and challenges and the modest budgets and the problems—the difficulties in it all—*you are involved in and attached to the greatest thing on this earth, the greatest thing that has ever been upon the face of this earth.*
>
> *You have the complete trust of the Brethren.* I say again that there is no greater evidence of the prophetic preparation of this people than the beginning of this religious education program, because when it was installed it was nice, but really not critically needed. It has had time to flourish and now helps to protect our youth from all that we face. . . . Be patient with all the realities that you face, all the difficulties and challenges. You brethren be understanding, be helpful to your lovely wives and companions, the mothers of your children. Sisters,

be patient with these brethren. They have chosen a better part. Encourage and sustain them. They are a *part of the greatest thing that transpires on this earth this day.*⁷⁶

Notes

1. This account is shared by Scott C. Esplin.
2. J. Reuben Clark Jr., "The Charted Course of the Church in Education," *Charge to Religious Educators*, 3rd ed. (Salt Lake City: The Church of Jesus Christ of Latter-day Saints, 1994), 4.
3. Boyd K. Packer, "The Mantle Is Far, Far Greater Than the Intellect," in *Charge to Religious Educators*, 3rd ed., 64; emphasis added.
4. Boyd K. Packer, "The Ideal Teacher," in *Charge to Religious Educators*, 3rd ed., 18.
5. Boyd K. Packer, "Teach the Scriptures," in *Charge to Religious Educators*, 3rd ed., 88.
6. Packer, "Teach the Scriptures," 88.
7. Ezra Taft Benson, in Conference Report, April 1987, 106.
8. Henry B. Eyring, "The Lord Will Multiply the Harvest," talk to the CES (Salt Lake City: The Church of Jesus Christ of Latter-day Saints, 1998), 1–2; all references cited as "talk to the CES" had limited distribution to CES teachers and leaders.
9. Boyd K. Packer, "Seek Learning Even by Study and Also by Faith," in *That All May Be Edified* (Salt Lake City: Bookcraft, 1982), 44.
10. Henry B. Eyring, "'And Thus We See': Helping a Student in a Moment of Doubt," in *Charge to Religious Educators*, 3rd ed., 107.
11. Marion G. Romney, "The Charted Course Reaffirmed," talk to the CES (Salt Lake City: The Church of Jesus Christ of Latter-day Saints, 1980), 1.
12. Eyring, "'And Thus We See': Helping a Student in a Moment of Doubt," 107.
13. Romney, "The Charted Course Reaffirmed," 1.
14. Mark E. Petersen, "Avoiding Sectarianism," in *Charge to Religious Educators*, 2nd ed. (Salt Lake City: The Church of Jesus Christ of Latter-day Saints, 1982), 118; emphasis added.
15. Clark, "The Charted Course," 6; emphasis added.
16. Clark, "The Charted Course," 7; emphasis added.
17. Bruce R. McConkie, "The Foolishness of Teaching," talk to the CES (Salt Lake City: The Church of Jesus Christ of Latter-day Saints, 1981), 13.

18. Jeffrey R. Holland, "Our Consuming Mission," talk to the CES (Salt Lake City: The Church of Jesus Christ of Latter-day Saints, 1999), 6.
19. Petersen, "Avoiding Sectarianism," 118.
20. Harold B. Lee, "Loyalty," in *Charge to Religious Educators*, 2nd ed., 64.
21. Packer, "The Mantle Is Far, Far Greater Than the Intellect," 65.
22. "Basic Doctrine," in *Charge to Religious Educators*, 3rd ed., 85.
23. Petersen, "Avoiding Sectarianism," 118.
24. McConkie, "The Foolishness of Teaching," 6.
25. Spencer W. Kimball, "The Ordinances of the Gospel," talk to the CES (Salt Lake City: The Church of Jesus Christ of Latter-day Saints, 1962), 24.
26. James E. Faust, "A Legacy of the New Testament," talk to the CES (Salt Lake City: The Church of Jesus Christ of Latter-day Saints, 1988), 2.
27. Jeffrey R. Holland, "Our Consuming Mission," talk to the CES (Salt Lake City: The Church of Jesus Christ of Latter-day Saints, 1999), 3.
28. Clark, "The Charted Course," 8.
29. Henry B. Eyring, "We Must Raise Our Sights," 2001 CES Conference, August 14, 2001, 3.
30. Neal A. Maxwell, "Glorify Christ," Evening with a General Authority address to CES, February 2, 2001, 1.
31. Marion G. Romney, untitled address to CES coordinators convention, April 13, 1973, 8.
32. Marion G. Romney, "The Value of a Well-Informed Faith," talk to the CES (Salt Lake City: The Church of Jesus Christ of Latter-day Saints, 1975), 10.
33. Clark, "The Charted Course," 6.
34. Boyd K. Packer, "To Those Who Teach in Troubled Times," in *Charge to Religious Educators*, 3rd ed., 100–1.
35. Packer, "To Those Who Teach," 101–2.
36. Spencer W. Kimball, "Men of Example," in *Charge to Religious Educators*, 3rd ed., 25–27.
37. Ezra Taft Benson, "The Gospel Teacher and His Message," *in Charge to Religious Educators*, 3rd ed., 11, 15.
38. Neal A. Maxwell, "But a Few Days," talk to the CES (Salt Lake City: The Church of Jesus Christ of Latter-day Saints, 1983), 2.
39. Joseph Smith, *History of the Church of Jesus Christ of Latter-day Saints*, ed. B. H. Roberts (Salt Lake City: The Church of Jesus Christ of Latter-day Saints, 1932–51), 1:64; emphasis added.

40. Noah Webster, *An American Dictionary of the English Language* (New York: S. Converse, 1828), s.v. "article"; emphasis added.
41. Petersen, "Avoiding Sectarianism," 118.
42. Jeffrey R. Holland, "Teaching Skills," talk to the CES (Salt Lake City: The Church of Jesus Christ of Latter-day Saints, 1992), 1–2; emphasis added.
43. Neal A. Maxwell, "Teaching by the Spirit—The Language of Inspiration," in *Charge to Religious Educators*, 3rd ed., 61.
44. Clark, "The Charted Course," 7.
45. Clark, "The Charted Course," 7.
46. McConkie, "The Foolishness of Teaching," 10.
47. Richard G. Scott, "Helping Others to Be Spiritually Led," talk to the CES (Salt Lake City: The Church of Jesus Christ of Latter-day Saints, 1998), 3.
48. Benson, "The Gospel Teacher and His Message," 14.
49. Henry B. Eyring, "Teaching the Old Testament," talk to the CES (Salt Lake City: The Church of Jesus Christ of Latter-day Saints, 1999), 1.
50. Henry B. Eyring, "A Miracle Required," talk to the CES administrators (Salt Lake City: The Church of Jesus Christ of Latter-day Saints, 1981), 12–13.
51. Jeffrey R. Holland, "Therefore, What?" 2000 CES Conference, August 8, 2000, 2.
52. Eyring, "We Must Raise Our Sights," 1.
53. Benson, "The Gospel Teacher and His Message," 13.
54. Eyring, "The Lord Will Multiply the Harvest," 4.
55. Eyring, "The Lord Will Multiply the Harvest," 6.
56. Harold B. Lee, "The Mission of Church Schools," talk to the CES (Salt Lake City: The Church of Jesus Christ of Latter-day Saints, 1953), 5.
57. Howard W. Hunter, "Eternal Investments," talk to the CES (Salt Lake City: The Church of Jesus Christ of Latter-day Saints, 1989), 2.
58. See Kimball, "The Ordinances of the Gospel," 6; and Thomas S. Monson, "True Shepherds after the Way of the Lord," in *Charge to Religious Educators*, 2nd ed., 78.
59. A. Theodore Tuttle, "Men with a Message," talk to the CES (Salt Lake City: The Church of Jesus Christ of Latter-day Saints, 1958), 83–84; emphasis added.
60. Spencer W. Kimball, "What I Hope You Will Teach My Grandchildren," talk to the CES (Salt Lake City: The Church of Jesus Christ of Latter-day Saints, 1966), 11.
61. A. Theodore Tuttle, "Teaching the Word to the Rising Generation," in *Charge to Religious Educators*, 2nd ed., 130.

62. Holland, "Therefore, What?" 7.
63. Neal A. Maxwell, "The Gospel Gives Answers to Life's Problems," in *Charge to Religious Educators,* 2d ed., 93.
64. Eyring, "A Miracle Required," 7, 12.
65. Eyring, "A Miracle Required," 13.
66. McConkie, "The Foolishness of Teaching," 8.
67. L. Tom Perry, "If Ye Receive Not the Spirit Ye Shall Not Teach," in *Book of Mormon Symposium Speeches* (Salt Lake City: The Church of Jesus Christ of Latter-day Saints, 1986), 34.
68. Richard G. Scott, "Four Fundamentals for Those Who Teach and Inspire Youth," in *Old Testament Symposium Speeches* (Salt Lake City: The Church of Jesus Christ of Latter-day Saints, 1987), 1–2.
69. Maxwell, "Teaching by the Spirit—The Language of Inspiration," 58–59.
70. Eyring, "Teaching the Old Testament," 6.
71. Neal A. Maxwell, "Those Seedling Saints Who Sit before You," in *Charge to Religious Educators*, 3rd ed., 31.
72. Henry B. Eyring, "Love and Loyalty," introduction to talk to the CES by Jeffrey R. Holland, "Our Consuming Mission" (Salt Lake City: The Church of Jesus Christ of Latter-day Saints, 1999).
73. Hunter, "Eternal Investments," 1; emphasis in original.
74. Eyring, "'And Thus We See': Helping a Student in a Moment of Doubt," 104.
75. Richard G. Scott, typescript of untitled video address to CES, February 4, 1994.
76. Packer, "Teach the Scriptures," 91–92; emphasis added.

As the Master Teacher, Jesus asked great questions that stirred the souls of men.

© Intellectual Reserve, Inc.

How to Ask Questions That Invite Revelation

Alan R. Maynes

Alan R. Maynes *is the Utah East Area Director in Price, Utah.*

"To ask and to answer questions is at the heart of all learning and teaching."[1]

When gospel teachers create a desire to learn in the minds and hearts of their students, revelation can come more readily. This is especially true when the inquiring students are led to discover principles of the gospel that have power to change their lives.

Jesus the Master Teacher

As the supreme model of master teaching, Jesus asked great questions that stirred the souls of men. His questions caused listeners to think and created within them a desire to know truth. The four Gospels have over 125 different questions that Jesus used to teach, lift, and inspire. His questions caused the truths of the gospel to sink deep into the hearts and minds of His listeners. As you read through the following examples, ponder how great, and yet how simple, each question is. Notice how they invite revelation on the part of the learner.

"Ye are the salt of the earth: but if the salt have lost his savour, wherewith shall it be salted?" (Matthew 5:13).

"For if ye love them which love you, what reward have ye?" (Matthew 5:46).

"What thinkest thou, Simon?" (Matthew 17:25).

"Dost thou believe on the Son of God?" (John 9:35).

"Lovest thou me more than these?" (John 21:15).

Jesus's questions are not limited to His mortal ministry but encompass His premortal, mortal, and postmortal teachings. Looking at the questions He poses causes one to think, "Why does the Lord ask questions when He knows all of our thoughts?" The answer is because this method is one of the most effective ways to help people to think, to consider, and to believe. Elder Henry B. Eyring said, "Some questions invite inspiration. Great teachers ask those."[2]

This article will explore the value of asking questions that invite revelation, present some thoughts on developing the talent of asking such questions, and finally, suggest methods of implementation in the classroom.

The Value of Asking Questions

Increasing student desire to learn. Questions can do many different things for students. In the first place, they can increase a student's desire to learn. When a student desires to learn, most behavioral problems will disappear. Although many students do come with a desire to learn, some need to have their desire increased. Often, they go through the motions of learning, but their minds are elsewhere. Questions can cause them to engage in the learning process because they encourage students to think. And, as Elder Robert D. Hales taught, "We must require our students to think."[3] When a student ponders the doctrine, exciting things happen. This excitement is contagious and affects everything else that happens in a classroom.

Increasing student participation. "Asking good questions and directing effective discussions are primary ways to encourage . . . participation."[4] As the interest level increases and answers are explored, students find they are enjoying, as well as learning. This participation is brought about when the teacher adopts a student focus.[5] For the gospel to reach down deep into their hearts and minds, students need to be truly interested in discovering eternal truths. Thought-provoking questions help bring this deeper level of participation.

Measuring student understanding. Asking great questions allows a teacher to measure a student's understanding. As students answer, the teacher can assess what the class does or does not understand. "You gain this measure of your students by listening to their response to your questions."[6] A teacher can teach above or below the level of student knowledge, which, in either case, causes boredom. The response from students allows a teacher to make maximum use of the allotted time by clearly covering those items not yet understood. It also brings all the students to an understanding of the principles being taught. The law of witnesses is applied as students validate to each other the gospel truth being considered.

Inviting revelation into students' lives. Elder Gene R. Cook taught, "The single greatest thing a teacher does is provide the environment in which people can have a spiritual experience."[7] Questions are essential in creating the necessary environment in the gospel classroom because they prepare the minds and hearts of the students. As the students participate, they authorize and therefore enable the Holy Ghost to teach them personally.[8] This occurs because the students exercise agency, and as they seek learning by faith, eternal truths can be discovered and internalized.

Questions help create a climate for the Spirit to come and witness to the truth. The Holy Ghost, thus invited, teaches students personally and individually. No wonder the Master Teacher, Jesus Christ, used questions so extensively to instruct and save the souls of men.

Developing the Talent of Asking Great Questions

The art of teaching. Some teaching talent comes as a gift, and some skills are acquired through instruction and practice. The appropriate use of great questions is at the center of effective teaching. It is worth every effort for a gospel teacher to develop this skill and hone it to perfection. Developing this skill requires asking the right questions during lesson preparation, not just lesson presentation.

Teacher preparation questions. This process begins with those questions a teacher asks while preparing a lesson, questions like "What was the author's intent?" "What are the most essential principles or doctrines?" "What do I want my students to know from this scripture block?" "What are the redeeming, the converting, or the life-changing principles?" Asking the proper questions during preparation invites revelation for several reasons. First, teachers will be guided as they humbly seek answers by the power of the Holy Ghost. Second, as Elder Eyring taught, "If you teach doctrinal principles the Holy Ghost will come."[9]

For years the Brethren have told us to teach Church doctrine, to teach those things taught by the prophets and apostles.[10] They have told us to be "cautious and restrained and totally orthodox in all matters of Church doctrine,"[11] to teach "truth[s] of eternal significance,"[12] and to avoid "fried froth"[13] or "minutia and insignificant things."[14] President Boyd K. Packer taught, "True doctrine, understood, changes attitudes and behavior."[15] If teachers are looking for the nonessential, insignificant tidbits and facts or a "theological Twinkie,"[16] that is what they will find. However, when teachers offer "students the benefit of a broader view,"[17]—looking for the intent of the inspired writer, the life-changing and converting principles that apply to the students—the Holy Ghost will accompany their study. Therefore, gospel teachers should "stay in the heart of the mine where the real gold is."[18] Then the power of the Spirit promised to gospel teachers can distill upon them as a gift from heaven. This endowment of the Spirit comes because "the Holy Ghost's job is to testify of truths of eternal significance."[19]

Being guided by the Spirit in *what to teach* is the place for a teacher to begin developing the ability to ask great questions. Looking for the important, the essential principles and doctrines will draw a teacher close to God. During His mortal ministry, Jesus focused His teachings on the basic principles of the gospel, and the Brethren likewise follow this pattern. Gospel teachers should do the same. When the teacher focuses on essential principles and doctrines, keeping the students in mind, the Holy Ghost is invited into the preparation process.

Searching questions. The Lord has given commandments to search the scriptures (see D&C 1:37; John 5:39; 3 Nephi 23:1; Joshua 1:8). Excitement comes into the life of one who discovers truths in the scriptures when guided by the Spirit. If a teacher can create that same experience for the students in the classroom, then learning is magnified many times over. That which students discover for themselves is much more life-changing and useful than that which they are told by someone else. One of the easiest ways to give the students this experience is to have them look for answers in the scriptures.

There are many ways to get students to search. Invite them to look for words, phrases, lists, meanings, additional information, understanding, principles, and doctrines. Avoid yes-no responses and obvious answers. Learning *what* to have students look for and *how* to invite them to look are skills that need careful consideration. Looking for the trivial or no-brainer information will not engage the mind. There will be times when a teacher will ask students to look for simple facts, but having them look for principles of truth, for understanding, and for application is more engaging. The invitation to search works best if it is given first, *before* the scripture is read.[20] Students will get more out of their reading because they are looking for something and will have questions in their minds: Where is it? What is it? What does it mean? Some words that will work well are "look for," "search for," "find," "underline," "mark," and "identify."

The clearer the invitation is, the more effective the search activity becomes. If there are several things being looked for, it helps to list the items on the board. Consider the following examples: "Look for what is unusual about the money system in Alma 10–12" or "Identify how Amulek could discern Zeezrom's thoughts in Alma 12:7." This information is nice to know, but it is not life-changing. A more engaging approach would be: "Students, look in Alma 10:31 and find out who was the foremost to accuse Amulek. Now look in Alma 15:12 and find out who is being baptized. Now let's look for what Alma and Amulek taught that changed Zeezrom. Using the following verses, Alma 12:25, 26, 30, 32, 33, look for what Zeezrom was taught that changed his life." Once students find the phrase "the plan of redemption," then have them look for what we learn about the plan from Alma and Amulek's teachings. This second example is more engaging because it focuses on that which is life-changing and converting. By searching this way, students can explore and discover principles of eternal significance that can be applied in their lives.

Analytical questions. Jesus knows the thoughts and intents of all our hearts, but seldom can teachers discern the thoughts of their students. When a student answers a question, a teacher can see a little better what students believe, understand, and feel. Parents, teachers, and leaders often say the youth know because they have been taught. I have been amazed when years later I find out my own children did not understand something as deeply and thoroughly as I would have hoped. Two way communication is one of the best ways to measure student comprehension. In the classroom, this is accomplished by asking simple questions that encourage and allow students to participate. The following phrases can assist a teacher in writing analytical questions:

What did you find . . . ?	What does it mean . . . ?
Why is that . . . ?	Why do you think . . . ?
In your opinion . . . ?	What evidence . . . ?
How do you think . . . ?	What are some ways . . . ?
How is it that . . . ?	What differences . . . ?

These questions are necessary to bring all to an understanding. Let us look again at Alma 11–12. After students have searched selected verses for Alma and Amulek's teaching of the plan of redemption, a teacher could ask: What did you find? What do you think that means? If the students' ideas are written on the board, the teacher can then ask: Which of those eternal truths listed on the board do you think affected Zeezrom the most? Why? Other questions could include: Why do you think Alma used the word *redemption* to describe the plan? How is it that an understanding of the plan of redemption causes change? These questions allow a teacher to see where the students are in their understanding. They help students to ponder the significance of what they are studying. Students are more able to internalize ideas as they are thoroughly discussed and explored. Questions also give students the opportunity to share and teach.[21] Asking this type of question requires a teacher who is willing to spend the time necessary to help all come to an understanding.

Application questions. Application questions or invitations are given to help students apply principles and doctrines in their own lives. In many classes, this invitation is not needed because the students have become so engaged and because understanding is so complete that the application happens spontaneously. If for some reason it does not, a simple question will suffice. Questions that begin with the following wording open the floodgates:

What have you learned . . . ?	What difference would it make . . . ?
When have you felt . . . ?	What do you feel/think God wants . . . ?
Share a time or experience	What does the Lord expect or desire . . . ?

Application questions give students the opportunity to explain what they have learned and what they feel God would like them to do. They help to bridge the gap between the scriptural account and their lives today. This process helps students find answers to their problems in the scriptures. It also allows them to share heartfelt feelings, which have a tremendous impact on their classmates.

Consider again Alma 10–12. Ask students, "What have you learned today that would help you come closer to the Savior?" This question personalizes the lesson. It causes students to think and take a little inventory of their personal standing before God. Other questions could be: "When have you felt that the plan of redemption caused change in your own life?" "What do you feel God wants you to do to take full advantage of the plan of redemption?" Ask the students to ponder the question or even write their response before answering. Some might be invited to share. This process of asking a question that causes them to apply the principle takes eternal truths deep into the hearts and minds of the students.

The path to student discovery. When students accept invitations to think and learn, the vault of divine knowledge is discovered and opened. Revelation is invited into hearts and minds. This can happen to the teacher during preparation and to the students and teacher during the course of the lesson. This type of teaching is very enjoyable and engaging for the teacher. Students have an edifying experience because it is so engaging and Spirit directed. It sounds rather simple and easy, and in many ways it is. It can also be difficult and challenging. It takes work, effort, and a lot of practice! The most important aspect of utilizing questions to teach is that students learn how to discover gospel truths for themselves. In order to teach this way, the teacher needs to be guided by the Spirit. The Spirit directs the *what*: the verses and principles that are to be searched. The Spirit also directs the *how*: the questions asked, when, to whom, and how students should be asked to respond.

Thus four types of questions are used: (1) preparation questions, (2) searching questions that invite students to look for information, (3) analytical questions that cause students to think and to evaluate, and (4) application questions that allow students to liken scriptures to themselves. These four types of questions have a logical sequence that leads to discovery.

Some fear that this logic and order in teaching is confining and lacks variety. I have had many teachers report that it is uncomfortable at first. Yet after some practice these same teachers report that it is liberating and inspiring. No longer do they ask the question, "What will I do tomorrow?" Instead, the teacher searches the assigned reading, prayerfully selecting what he or she feels will be the most beneficial to students. The teacher then prepares the questions that cause the students to search for information, analyze that information, and make application. There are many other things that a gospel teacher will do and use in the classroom, such as visuals, stories, role-plays, lectures, and so forth. However, these fundamental questions provide a great framework to build an engaging lesson.

I have visited hundreds of classrooms, and the effect of powerful questions is incredible. To sit in a class where students are willing, excited, and engaged and where they are participating, discovering, sharing, teaching, and even testifying is almost indescribable. The thoughts that enter my mind are: "Oh, if my son or daughter could be in this class!" "I wish every young person could have this experience." "Every seminary and institute class should be like this." The talent of questioning is worth any effort to develop so that revelation is invited into our classrooms and into the hearts and minds of each student and teacher.

Implementation

Because teaching is so habitual, we may seem to go on automatic pilot when we stand in front of the class. Teachers practice every day, several times a day. The abilities, strengths, and talents that have been developed over the years become very evident. The teachers' weaknesses are also easily observed. Therefore, it takes great effort, along with a plan of action, to change and improve. These changes must be sustained over a long enough period of time that the old habits and practices are replaced. Often it is uncomfortable when a new idea is tried. Many throw their hands in the air and say, "It does not fit my personality" or "That didn't work for me." An appreciation and understanding of the power that habits have in our lives can give a teacher the fortitude to choose to improve and to grow and develop in acquiring new teaching skills.

How to improve. The more a person treads a path, the firmer the path becomes. One key to changing our teaching style is to prepare a lesson plan with effective questions. If a teacher cannot write a good question in the quiet of the office, there is little chance a good question will come out when the teacher is standing before a class. The process of thinking and writing facilitates improvement and change. Three well-written questions for each lesson can do wonders. In fact, the process of writing great questions can affect the logic and thinking of the teacher so profoundly that all the questions a teacher asks begin to improve.

How to teach with questions. The teacher does not just stand up and ask one question after another; the experience is one of searching, discussing, discovering, sharing, and teaching. It is very edifying. The teacher needs to decide things like: Do we discuss together as a class, in groups, in pairs, or alone? Do I tell the story or background, or have students tell, or do we discover together?

We all know that friends and peers have a powerful effect in the students' lives. Because of this high level of peer influence, when students share responses to questions and teach each other, it is especially effective. One of the best ways to get students to share and teach each other is to ask a question and have them respond to the class, to a group, or to a partner. For example, the answers to the questions "Which part of the plan do you think affected Zeezrom the most? Why?" could be shared and discussed as a class, in small groups, or in pairs. The question could also be asked this way: "Which part of the plan do you think the youth of the Church need to understand today?" As students share their answers, they are influencing each other—they are teaching each other. President Packer taught that "a testimony is to be *found* in the *bearing* of it!"[22] Because of the students' participation, the Spirit can witness to the individual that what he or she is saying is true. It can also witness to their partner, their group, or the entire class. This causes the students to feel more deeply about what they have learned and come to believe. They *know* that they *know*, and they feel that they know. Therefore, they come to realize that they do have a testimony and that it is good.

Conclusion

Increasing student participation does have a few challenges. The manner in which student comments are received affects the success of every question that is asked. A teacher needs to have high regard for the students. The students need to feel that their comments are valued and appreciated. Likewise, a teacher cannot accept all opinions as truth but must guide the class to the proper conclusions. It takes some practice and especially a love for students to graciously receive their answers and still maintain doctrinal purity. When the Spirit is present and effective questions are being explored, they will create and draw out thoughts, ideas, and additional questions from the students. A teacher should not be too rigid but should be open to guidance so that the Spirit is directing the teaching and learning.

Consider the following from Elder Cecil O. Samuelson: "I marvel each time I consider the wonderful way in which the Prophet Joseph Smith used proper questions not only to enhance his knowledge but also to enlarge his faith. . . . The question is not whether we should ask questions but rather, What are the questions we should be asking? My experience in science and medicine leads me to believe that real progress is almost always the result of asking the right questions."[23] My experience has also led me to believe that if we are to make real progress in taking the gospel deeper into the hearts and minds of the students, we need to be asking the "right questions," even questions that invite revelation. If we are to fulfill the charge to "raise our sights" and have our students "become truly converted to the restored gospel of Jesus Christ while they are with us,"[24] we must create a climate in which the Holy Ghost can come and teach with great power and change our hearts. Great questions are vital in bringing this to pass. I know that this skill can be acquired over time, through diligent effort and practice. Just as a marvelous flood of light came forth as the Prophet Joseph Smith asked great questions, so can that much-needed light flood into the hearts and minds of gospel teachers and students everywhere as we seek the Lord's help in improving our ability to ask questions that invite revelation.

Notes

1. Henry B. Eyring, "The Lord Will Multiply the Harvest," address to religious educators, February 6, 1998 (Salt Lake City: The Church of Jesus Christ of Latter-day Saints, 1998), 5.
2. Eyring, "The Lord Will Multiply the Harvest," 5.
3. Robert D. Hales, "Teaching by Faith," address to religious educators, February 1, 2002 (Salt Lake City: The Church of Jesus Christ of Latter-day Saints, 2002), 3.
4. *Teaching the Gospel: A Handbook for CES Teachers and Leaders* (Salt Lake City: The Church of Jesus Christ of Latter-day Saints, 1994), 37.
5. See *Teaching the Gospel*, 13.
6. Hales, "Teaching by Faith," 6.
7. Gene R. Cook, *Teaching by the Spirit* (Salt Lake City: Deseret Book, 2000), 192.
8. Richard G. Scott, "Helping Others to Be Spiritually Led," address given at the Church Educational System Symposium, August 11, 1998 (Salt Lake City: The Church of Jesus Christ of Latter-day Saints, 1998), 2–3.
9. Henry B. Eyring, CES satellite training broadcast, August 10, 2003
10. J. Reuben Clark Jr., "The Charted Course of the Church in Education," in *Charge to Religious Educators*, 3rd ed. (Salt Lake City: The Church of Jesus Christ of Latter-day Saints, 1994), 7.
11. Jeffrey R. Holland, "We Are Teachers of the Gospel," introduction to "An Evening with Gordon B. Hinckley," September 15, 1978.
12. Eyring, CES satellite training broadcast, August 10, 2003.
13. Jeffrey R. Holland, in Conference Report, April 1998, 32.
14. Bruce R. McConkie, "Finding Answers to Gospel Questions," in *Charge to Religious Educators*, 79.
15. Boyd K. Packer, in Conference Report, October 1986, 20.
16. Holland, in Conference Report, April 1998, 32.

17. Jeffrey R. Holland, "Therefore, What?" address given at the Twenty-fourth Annual Church Educational System Religious Educators Conference, August 8, 2000 (Salt Lake City: The Church of Jesus Christ of Latter-day Saints, 2000), 2.
18. Holland, "Therefore, What?" 2.
19. Eyring, CES satellite training broadcast, August 10, 2003.
20. Robert Jones, "Asking Questions First," *Ensign*, January 2002, 24.
21. A Current Teaching Emphasis for the Church Educational System, letter dated April 4, 2003.
22. Boyd K. Packer, "The Candle of the Lord," *Ensign*, January 1983, 51–56.
23. Cecil O. Samuelson Jr., "The Importance of Asking Questions," *Brigham Young University 2001–2002 Speeches* (Provo, UT: Brigham Young University Press, 2002), 149–57.
24. Henry B. Eyring, "We Must Raise Our Sights," address at the Church Educational System Conference, August 14, 2001 (Salt Lake City: The Church of Jesus Christ of Latter-day Saints, 2001), 2.

An unrushed atmosphere is essential if we want to have the Spirit of the Lord in our classes.

© Intellectual Reserve, Inc.

Effective Classroom Time Management

Scott H. Knecht

Scott H. Knecht *is assistant to the area director of Seminaries and Institutes of Religion in Southern California.*

Of all the teacher's roles, one of the least discussed is timekeeper. Along with everything else, it almost seems silly that a teacher would have to assume this additional role. But if the teacher does not take the role of timekeeper, it is left undone. All class periods are bound by both a starting time and a stopping time, and within that framework a teacher needs to introduce an idea, encourage and allow for student learning in a variety of ways, and bring everything together in a way that helps students want to change for the better. Since we are bound by time, we should make time our friend instead of our enemy.

In the February 2007 worldwide leadership training meeting, Elder Jeffrey R. Holland said, "An unrushed atmosphere is absolutely essential if you are to have the Spirit of the Lord present in your class. Please don't ever forget that. Too many of us rush. We rush right past the Spirit of the Lord trying to beat the clock in some absolutely unnecessary footrace."[1] Teachers must be the creators and maintainers of that unrushed atmosphere, even as they guide their students to learning.

How many of these scenarios sound familiar?

• The class begins and the teacher starts by saying, "We have a lot of material to cover today, and I don't know if we have the time, so we will just do our best."

- The class is rolling along smoothly until ten to fifteen minutes before the end when the teacher notices the clock and in a panic says, "We are never going to get this all in," and then races to the end of class.
- The time to end the class has arrived, and the teacher is still talking. Now the time is past, and students are fidgeting, packing up their things, and starting to leave, one by one. The teacher pleads for them to stay to cover "just one more important point."

All these scenarios result from poor time management. When teachers cannot manage their time, the Spirit feels a little less welcome. Student learning suffers.

A friend, an excellent public schoolteacher, said, "Time does not belong solely to the teacher. For the moments we teach, ownership of time is shared jointly between us and our students. To think that it is solely our own is a gross misassumption." Teachers have an obligation as they plan their lessons to stay within the given time parameters, for their sake and for the students'. Obviously not all material will be addressed, taught, and learned, but part of the teacher's duty is "selective neglect," deciding which parts will receive attention and which will not. It is also not as important to cover material as it is to help your students personally uncover it. Generally a race against the clock covers more material, but this is a poor way for students to learn. Sometimes less is more. Consider these points:

- In gospel education, it probably will not be the only time that a student studies the book of scripture you are teaching in your course. Over a lifetime we will all cycle through the four standard works many times. Different principles and doctrines will be highlighted each time through, whether it is in a class or in personal study. It would be foolish to think that the burden of exposing students to everything in a block of scripture falls on one teacher in one class.
- An unspoken contract exists between teacher and student. Teachers generally like to start on time and want all of the students there to begin together. The flip side of the obligation is that students expect a teacher to end the class on time. Students have other duties to attend to—other classes, employment, study, social time, and so forth. When we as teachers do not uphold our end of the deal, we frustrate students, and the rising frustration level does not enhance the atmosphere.
- What would cause a teacher to go over time? Often teachers say they just lost track of time, which is understandably easy to do. The simple solution

is to remember that part of controlling the class is to control the pacing, so we need to make that part of what we do as teachers. Other reasons teachers gave for going over time are that the class was going so well or that the students were so engaged, it was just difficult to stop. In almost all those cases, I have observed that it was not so much the students but the teachers who were engaged in telling a story or sharing some of their thoughts and feelings with the class. When teachers hold a class over so that they can keep talking, the class generally has descended to teaching-as-telling, and that is a very ineffective way for students to learn.

Below are five ideas to make time your ally and not your enemy:

1. Think of timekeeping issues as you prepare your lesson. Ask yourself some of these questions: About how long do I think this discussion will go? What follow-up questions are likely to ensue from this main question? What are some of the points I hope will emerge from this activity? How much time do we need at the end of class to allow for effective application? And perhaps the most important question: What are we really trying to do in class today—cover a lot of material, or help students really learn some important principles and doctrines?

2. Make yourself aware of the time in a class. Learn to glance at the clock or your watch on a regular basis. Make some visible marks on your lesson plan of the approximate times that you expect to be at certain spots. Stay aware of where you are and where you would like to be.

3. Manage the discussion in class. Some students like to ramble and dominate the time. Learn to gently help them summarize and tighten things up. Do not be afraid to say things like, "Let's take just one more comment on this issue then move on." Every class seems to have some students who want to stay on a topic longer and some who have had enough. It is the teacher's job to keep the majority of the students engaged and interested so they will inquire and learn. That may require you to keep moving. Moving along is hard when students want to keep talking. We always seek more input from students, and we solicit more comments. When students begin to participate it always feels good, so it seems counterintuitive to stop taking comments on a subject in order to move on. But if the Spirit is in the class and the students are engaged, trust that when you move on to continue the learning process they will stay engaged, and they will begin to see links and connections between their own life and a variety of scriptural passages, principles, and doctrines.

4. Do not make negative statements about the time. Students rarely, if ever, know how much their teachers think they need to accomplish in a given period. We make time our enemy when we play slave to the clock, then verbalize it to the class ("Look at the time—there's never enough time!"). Be sufficiently aware of where you are so that students will have enough time to digest what is going on, and you will have enough to be able to challenge them to make positive changes, all within the framework of the allotted time. Announcing your frustration with the lack of time only serves to pass that frustration on to the students. They do not need it, and it does not help anything.

5. Always stay susceptible to the promptings of the Spirit. Our best efforts at planning and pacing may need to be revised when we hit a real point of testimony and power. The Spirit will tell us when that is, and we should learn to respond to it. But there are also times when the Spirit will suggest that we move on to be able to get to one of those points of testimony and power. The teacher has to summon the courage to lead the class to that point, even if it means shortening something else.

The ideal situation seems to be that we are able to create in the class a safe atmosphere in which students can ask, respond, create, testify, and change, all within the allotted time for the class. Some classes are fifty minutes, some ninety, and some two hours or more. The teacher who learns how to do all of that within the time allotted not only creates that "unrushed atmosphere" that Elder Holland speaks of, but also honors the time and agency of the students, thus edifying them. The more edified they feel, the easier it is to help them learn.

Note

1. Jeffrey R. Holland, "Teaching and Learning in the Church," *Ensign*, June 2007, 91.

Raising the Bar: Preparing Future Missionaries

Brent L. Top

Brent L. Top *is a professor of Church history and doctrine at BYU.*

On December 11, 2002, the First Presidency and the Quorum of the Twelve Apostles issued a remarkable statement on missionary work. At the time, most Church members did not realize how that statement and the subsequent changes in missionary efforts that resulted from it would revolutionize the latter-day work of proclaiming the gospel. The phrase "raising the bar" soon became common among members of the Church in describing the increased expectations for missionaries. Upon hearing the phrase, I, like most members of the Church, thought primarily of higher standards of moral worthiness to serve as a full-time missionary. Qualifications were certainly a significant part of the statement on missionary work. Moral worthiness and physical, mental, and emotional stability are certainly part of raising the bar. However, there are other aspects that are just as vital but are often overlooked and underemphasized. I came to view raising the bar much differently than I previously had and in a much more comprehensive manner when I was called to serve as a mission president. That responsibility and the total immersion in missionary matters—from the constant need for teaching, training, and motivating missionaries to assisting Church leaders and members in fulfilling their gospel-sharing responsibilities—caused me to look upon missionary preparation with new eyes.

For over thirty years I have been a religious educator—ten years with seminaries and institutes as a released-time seminary teacher and institute instructor and twenty years on the Religious Education faculty at Brigham Young University. I have always felt it an incredible privilege and sacred responsibility to teach the young men and women in my classes. Like you, I want my students to be stretched intellectually and strengthened spiritually. I want their knowledge of the scriptures and doctrines of the gospel expanded, their devotion to the Lord and His Church intensified, their testimonies fortified, and their lives, love, and service empowered. I must admit, however, that I have not always thought as deeply and specifically as I should have concerning the impact of my teaching in preparing them to be effective missionaries—both as full-time missionaries and as life-long member missionaries.

With the new eyes acquired through my mission experience, I now see more clearly that *all* of my students are not only prospective full-time missionaries but are already missionaries and will be throughout their lives. And knowing that, I now see that each class I am teaching—whether it be Book of Mormon, New Testament, Doctrine and Covenants, teachings of the living prophets, Church history, LDS marriage and family, or any of our wide array of courses—must be more directed to preparing what Elder M. Russell Ballard called "the greatest generation of missionaries in the history of the Church."[1] After discussing what is required of young men and women today to become that greatest generation of missionaries, Elder Ballard spoke specifically to fathers: "If we are 'raising the bar' for your sons [and daughters] to serve as missionaries, that means we are also 'raising the bar' for you. *If we expect more of them, that means we expect more of you.*"[2] I believe this principle applies not only to parents and Church leaders but also to us as religious educators. "This isn't a time for spiritual weaklings," Elder Ballard declared.[3] That applies to us as well. This isn't a time for "weak sauce" religious educators (a term my missionaries often used to describe something tentative, feeble, or lacking boldness and power). The bar has been raised for all of us.

"I Wish I Would Have"

Hundreds of times in my interviews with the missionaries, I heard sentiments expressed that began with the phrase "I wish I would have." Perhaps the most common expression was, "I wish I would have known how difficult a mission is." But there were many other similar expressions—"I wish I had studied the Book of Mormon more," "I wish I had paid more attention in seminary," "I wish I knew the scriptures better," "I wish I had formed better study habits," "I wish I understood the gospel more," "I wish my testimony was stronger." Upon arriving in the mission field, I observed some missionaries who struggled mightily with the transition from being a teenager to a full-time missionary. Yet others hit the ground running and almost immediately became confident, competent, and powerful teachers of the gospel. What is the difference? Why are some so well prepared and others not? Of course, there are a myriad of factors—almost as many as missionaries themselves. Yet there are some specific things I observed and experienced as a mission president that have caused me to rethink my teaching philosophy and retool my teaching methods.

Most of the several hundred young men and women who served in our mission had attended seminary. Fewer, but still a substantial number, had participated in institute classes. Even fewer had been enrolled in religion classes at the respective BYU campuses. I mention that fact to demonstrate that the primary religious educational experience of full-time missionaries in the Church today is found in seminary classes throughout the world—whether it be released-time, early-morning, or home-study. When I came to that realization, it gave me pause. I found myself expressing the "I wish I would have" sentiments I had so often heard from my missionaries. I wish I would have taught my seminary students more specifically and effectively those things that would have enabled them to become effective missionaries. I wish I would have seen more clearly that every student in my class is not just a prospective full-time missionary, but *is* already a missionary and *will be* a missionary all his or her life.

With my release as mission president, I returned to my teaching responsibilities at BYU. Although the courses I teach are the same as those I taught before my mission, I am different. With the new eyes acquired from the mission experience, I saw many things differently. For example, the standard works are the same, but what I see in them is different. Likewise, the students sitting in my classes look much the same today as four years ago (except they seem younger than they used to), but now I see them in a new light. As I envision them wearing black name badges and white shirts and ties or being confronted with missionary opportunities in the form of questions or challenges (as they all will inevitably be) two questions come into my mind now: (1) If this young man or young woman sitting before me were called to serve in my mission, what would I want him or her to know? (2) How can my teaching help them to "stand as witnesses of God at all times and in all things, and in all places" with more confidence, competence, and conviction? (Mosiah 18:9). My mind races when I think of all the things I would want them to know and attributes I would desire them to possess. Yet, for me, it seems to boil down to three main things I want my students—all my students, whether they are preparing to serve full-time missions or just striving to be good member missionaries—to know. Now, more fervently and urgently than ever before in my religious education career, I want my students to *know*: (1) the truthfulness of the gospel, (2) the doctrines of the gospel, and (3) how to share the gospel.

Know the Gospel Is True

"Your own personal testimony," President James E. Faust counseled missionaries, "is the strongest arrow in your quiver."[4] Because of that, all of our teaching must be to that end. "Begin with the end in mind," is a familiar saying that is particularly relevant, even vital, for religious educators. One of the missionary skills that we continually stressed to our missionaries was what we called "teaching to the commitment." That means that all we teach—every doctrine and every principle—must lead to extending a commitment to the investigators to become "doers of the word and not hearers only" (James 1:22). Every principle taught has a desired outcome or action that we desire those whom we teach to do and experience in their lives. It is not enough for missionaries to merely teach *about* the truths of the gospel. In fact, if that is all they do, they have lost (or never had) sight of what the Lord called them to do. Effective missionaries want those they teach to *know* and *live* those truths and *experience* the blessings that always come when they do so. In teaching about the Apostasy and Restoration, missionaries will invite investigators to read Joseph Smith's account of the First Vision or the introduction to the Book of Mormon and selected passages, ponder on that, and pray specifically to gain a testimony of the truthfulness of those events. They teach them specifically *what* it means to gain a testimony, *how* they can obtain one, and *why* that testimony will change their lives forever. It should be the same for religious educators. While we need not teach to the commitment exactly like a missionary does by extending invitations to action with every concept taught; we can, nonetheless, "teach for conversion" with every lesson, every discussion, and every assignment. How can we more effectively teach for conversion? I don't have all the answers, but here are a few things I learned as a mission president that I have tried to transfer to my teaching as a religious educator.

Important versus Interesting

If you are like me, you have far more lesson material than you have class time to adequately cover. As a result, we all have to make hard decisions—hopefully with good judgment and inspiration—as to what would be most important to spend valuable class time teaching and discussing. My desire to teach for conversion now causes me to regularly ask, "Will this strengthen testimony?" and "Does this contribute to conversion?"

Sometimes my missionaries would complain that a member with whom they were teaching investigators would teach peripheral things like polygamy, a mother in heaven, archaeological evidences for the Book of Mormon, becoming like God, "eternal increase," or any number of other things that the member personally found fascinating. It may have been interesting (and that is not always a good description) but rarely, if ever, was it helpful. Never once did I hear of someone being converted by such discussions. Instead of conviction, the investigator was usually left with confusion.

As irritating as that was to me as mission president, I must sadly admit that perhaps I have been guilty of much the same thing in my own teaching. Sometimes I may have focused more attention in my teaching on facts than faith—demonstrating how much I know—than on ensuring that my students *know* the right things—the salvationally significant things. "All knowledge is not of equal significance," Elder Neal A. Maxwell declared. "There is no democracy of facts! They are not of equal importance. Something might be factual but unimportant. . . . For instance, today I wear a dark blue suit. That is true, but it is unimportant. . . . As we brush against truth, we sense that it has a hierarchy of importance. . . . Some truths are salvationally significant, and others are not."[5] Perhaps at times in my seminary or institute classes or my religion classes at BYU I have placed more emphasis on student interest than student conversion. I think I understand better now what Elder William R. Bradford meant when he said, "Some things are interesting while other things are important."[6] None of us has time to teach everything that we know, that we personally find fascinating, or that would keep the sleepy, back-row early-morning-seminary students on the edge of their seat. What we can do, however, is strive a little harder to ensure that the interesting never crowds out or confuses the important, even the imperative.

Don't Assume They Know

Assumptions often get us into trouble. We probably have all had an experience where what we assumed to be so was not. As a mission president, I quickly realized that I could not assume that all arriving missionaries were worthy to be there. Once in a while there were some sad surprises. It was essential that I carefully interview every missionary, not only when they arrived but regularly thereafter. Likewise, I learned that I could not assume that all of my missionaries had burning testimonies of the gospel, either at their arrival or at the conclusion of their missions. Sometimes I was surprised to learn that an elder or sister who bore powerful testimony that first night in the mission home later doubted their testimony when encountering difficult questions, challenges, or persecution. I learned that, as with investigators, you cannot assume that missionaries know what a testimony is, what you must do to gain (and retain) one, or how you know when you really know. These concepts are basic but are often taken for granted. They need to be taught, retaught, and retaught because missionaries, like investigators, need to gain and retain their testimonies every day as they encounter new challenges, new questions, and new circumstances.

In a similar manner, we cannot assume that our students—whether they are fourteen or forty—have testimonies of the gospel. And we certainly must not assume that they *all* know how to acquire a testimony or that they know how they will know when they have one. Likewise, we cannot assume that having a general testimony (an "I love the gospel" testimony) is the same as a specific testimony—an unmistakable witness by the power of the Holy Ghost of the truthfulness of a specific doctrine like the cleansing and transforming power of the Atonement of Jesus Christ, Joseph Smith's First Vision, the restoration of the priesthood, the truthfulness of the Book of Mormon, the Church as "the only true and living church upon the face of the whole earth" (D&C 1:30), and the fact that we are indeed led today by living prophets and apostles. The investigators that best progressed toward baptism and the new converts that were retained and progressed toward the temple were those who prayed for and received *specific* testimonies. In this way, they are continually "nourished by the good word of God" and empowered to continue as disciples of Christ (Moroni 6:4; see also John 8:31). And so it will be with our students—and each of us. Specific testimonies, repeatedly acquired by the power of the Holy Ghost, lead to staying power. President Harold B.

Lee taught: "Testimony isn't something you have today, and you are going to have always. A testimony is fragile. It is as hard to hold as a moonbeam. It is something you have to recapture every day of your life."[7]

Just as missionaries always invite investigators to come to know for themselves the truth concerning the *specific* things they learn and study, we must not neglect to do the same with our students. We cannot merely assume that they will do so. In the April 2008 general conference, Elder Dallin H. Oaks provided us powerful instruction concerning testimonies. He not only taught us what a testimony is and how it is obtained, but he also taught us how we can share our testimonies with others. As I listened to his words, I felt impressed that I, as a religious educator, need to review his instruction each semester with my students and discuss how it applies to the very doctrines and principles that we will study in the course. This is one way whereby I can ensure that I don't simply assume things that may not be so. It is also a means whereby I help future missionaries to fill their spiritual quivers with their strongest arrows.

Know the Doctrines of the Gospel

As teachers of the gospel, we are very familiar with President Boyd K. Packer's statement concerning the power of pure doctrine. "True doctrine, understood, changes attitudes and behavior," he taught. "The study of the doctrines of the gospel will improve behavior quicker than a study of behavior will improve behavior."[8] I have personally read and used that statement in my teaching scores of times. I thought I knew it and believed it. It was as a mission president, however, that I observed and experienced, in dramatic ways, the transforming power of doctrine. Knowing, teaching, and living the foundational doctrines of the restored gospel transformed the mission, the missionaries, the members, and the investigators. We experienced in our mission something akin to what Alma described regarding his missionary and reactivation efforts among the Zoramites. "And now, as the preaching of the word [that is, teaching doctrine] had a great tendency to lead the people to do that which was just—yea, it had had a more powerful effect upon the minds of the people than the sword, or anything else, which had happened to them—therefore Alma thought it was expedient that they should try the virtue of the word of God" (Alma 31:5). Truly, doctrine changed behaviors and attitudes within our mission. The virtue of the word of God powerfully led our missionaries "to do that which was just," resulting in strengthened spirituality, improved obedience, increased work ethic, and more persuasive gospel teaching.

One of the most significant changes that came as a result of the statement on missionary work and the subsequent release of *Preach My Gospel* was the elimination of memorized lesson presentations. "Our purpose is to teach the message of the restored gospel in such a way as to allow the Spirit to direct both the missionaries and those being taught," the First Presidency and Quorum of the Twelve Apostles declared. Missionaries were instructed to "not give a memorized recitation, but speak from the heart . . . out of [their] own conviction and in [their] own words."[9] To teach in one's own words, out of one's heart of conviction, and by the power of the Spirit, missionaries are specifically instructed in *Preach My Gospel* to seek "a deep knowledge of the doctrine."[10] To assist them in that objective, *Preach My Gospel* provides invaluable instruction for missionaries and members alike in the "essential doctrines, principles, and commandments that you are to study, believe, love, live, and teach."[11]

Knowing the doctrine—inside and out, broad and deep—is imperative in becoming "the greatest generation of missionaries." Raising the bar requires increased gospel knowledge on the part of all prospective missionaries. The Lord promised that the Spirit will give us "in the very hour" what we should teach, but only *if* we "treasure up in [our] minds continually the words of life" (D&C 84:85). Missionaries effectively teach by the Spirit only after they have treasured up knowledge of the doctrines of the kingdom. That places a greater responsibility upon the shoulders of all religious educators to likewise raise the bar in our teaching of doctrine. Each of us can probably think of many ways in which we can do that. I know there are many areas in which I need to improve, but my experience with using *Preach My Gospel* to train full-time missionaries and member missionaries has caused me to focus on two specific ways that I can better help my students treasure up the doctrines.

Connect the Dots

Within the first few days after arriving in the mission field, I attended a series of district meetings where I observed our missionaries teaching one another the lessons. There were things that I heard that were encouraging and impressive, but there were also many things that discouraged me. One of the most common deficiencies that I observed was that the elders and sisters could recite the basic principles of the missionary lessons but lacked the depth of understanding to be able to adequately explain those principles or answer questions about them. It was almost like they were giving the investigators a thousand pieces of a puzzle, but little help in showing how they fit together to form a beautiful picture. I realized that these missionaries were not all that different from our students (and perhaps a large segment of the general Church membership). It is common for us to pack in our bags of doctrinal knowledge lots of snippets of information—facts, scripture references, inspirational stories, quotes, basic teachings, things we have heard in classes and quorums through the years. What is far less common (at least among the missionaries with whom I served) is the ability to connect the dots. Do you remember drawing a picture, as a child, by connecting the numbered dots? The dots by themselves didn't reveal much. When connected, however, a delightful picture emerged. It works the same way with the doctrines of the gospel. Missionaries do disservice to their investigators if they only teach dots—isolated, unconnected, independent teachings. Real understanding and ultimate conversion comes when they connect the dots and see the big picture—the panoramic view of the great plan of happiness. *Preach My Gospel* helps the missionaries see those connections—the relationships between the principles and ordinances of the gospel and how each fits in the overall gospel plan. In addition to teaching *what* we believe, it gives us the reason *why* we believe it. For example, we can teach *what* the Restoration was, but understanding *why* it was necessary requires a connection to the Great Apostasy.

Another illustrative example would be teaching the first principles and ordinances of the gospel. Much can be taught about the *whats* of faith, repentance, baptism, and the gift of the Holy Ghost. But the real power—the converting power—of these doctrines is found in their relationship to each other and their absolute connection to the Atonement of Jesus Christ. You can't truly understand repentance without connecting it to faith. Interestingly, Amulek demonstrated this teaching method when he taught us about "faith *unto* repentance" not merely faith *and* repentance as separate doctrines (Alma 34:15; see also vv. 16–17). The *Preach My Gospel* pattern of gospel teaching by missionaries to investigators (and others) can, likewise, enhance our teaching as religious educators and help our students connect the doctrinal dots.

Doctrinal instruction comprised a significant portion of every zone conference in our mission. Using the doctrines taught in the missionary lessons (found in chapter 3 of *Preach My Gospel*), my wife and I sought to help the missionaries better understand not only all of the different dimensions of a specific doctrine but also how that doctrine is interconnected with and logically leads to the other doctrines we teach. It was exciting and gratifying to see the reactions of our missionaries. The lights were turned on—almost as if it was the first time that they really got it. When missionaries connect the dots, their testimonies are strengthened, their gospel knowledge deepens, and their ability to teach others with clarity and conviction improves. Because of these experiences, I realize more than ever that helping prospective missionaries see the big picture of the plan of salvation and connect the dots of the doctrines of the gospel will enable them to hit the ground running as full-time missionaries and will bless their lives forever.

Teach Them How to Study the Gospel

Virtually all of the missionaries we served with had read the Book of Mormon prior to their mission—most of them had read it more than once. They hardly ever missed reading their scriptures, a habit often started in seminary. That is great news, but the flip side is not so good. One of the most common deficiencies I recognized among our missionaries was the lack of gospel and scripture study skills. To most, gospel study meant merely reading scriptures and approved Church books. In the years preceding their missions, there had been considerable emphasis on daily scripture reading and getting through a volume of scripture, but very little instruction on ways to effectively and deeply *study* the doctrines of the gospel. Many, if not most, of our missionaries were familiar with scripture mastery passages, often having at least some of those passages memorized. Yet they could not adequately explain the very passages they had committed to memory and rarely understood the scriptural context for them.

Since most of our missionaries had never done a topical or doctrinal study of any of the standard works, I introduced to them a project that proved extraordinarily successful. It not only helped them learn how to study the scriptures by looking for specific doctrines, but also increased their knowledge of gospel principles (particularly those doctrines taught in the missionary lessons) and strengthened their personal testimonies and spirituality. I gave each of them a new missionary copy of the Book of Mormon and four different colored pencils. Each color represented one of the missionary lessons. Their assignment was to carefully study chapter three in *Preach My Gospel* and make a list of the main doctrines taught in each lesson. From that list of doctrines they then studied the Book of Mormon each day in their personal study, looking for specific principles taught in the missionary lessons and marking those passages with the appropriate color. They were amazed at what they found and how clearly the Book of Mormon taught those principles. Their pool of scriptures that could be used in teaching the lessons grew dramatically. Soon they were cross-referencing, writing notes in the margins, and sharing insights and applications with each other. It was exciting and gratifying to me to see their enthusiasm for scripture study. That enthusiasm, as well as what they were learning, became evident in their teaching. Their love for gospel study likewise affected their love for the work.

At an area mission presidents seminar, I found myself sitting at the lunch table with Elder Ballard and many other far more experienced mission presidents. Knowing that I was a religious educator by profession, Elder Ballard asked me how I had obtained my knowledge of the scriptures and doctrines of the gospel. I explained that virtually all I knew had come as I had prepared for teaching and prepared my lesson outlines. That, fortunately, was the point Elder Ballard wanted to make. Deep doctrinal knowledge—the kind of knowledge that is required to effectively teach others—rarely, if ever, comes just from reading. "Now, you need to get your missionaries to do the same thing," Elder Ballard stated. He was teaching us that missionaries increase their gospel knowledge when they prepare teaching outlines for the individuals they are teaching. I realized then that missionaries (in fact, all of us) need to study in preparation to teach, not just read, the scriptures. Fortunately, I didn't have to come up with ideas or programs to facilitate that. *Preach My Gospel* has the best ideas and is a missionary's best gospel study program.

Preach My Gospel contains arguably the best instruction on effective gospel study ever published by the Church. While directed primarily to missionaries, the suggestions found in chapter 2 will bless any student of the scriptures, including religious educators. As we raise the bar in our teaching efforts, we can use the principles taught, the scripture references to be studied, and the learning activities included in *Preach My Gospel* (particularly the study ideas and suggestions on pages 22–24) with our own students.

Modeling effective study skills in our teaching will enable our students to learn by observation and personal practice, not merely by hearing us talk about these principles. Each day in my classes, I try to utilize suggestions from *Preach My Gospel* and expect my students to do the same. Some of the more pertinent practices that we can more frequently model for our students in our classroom discussions could include:

- Ask yourself, "What is the author saying? What is the central message? How does this apply to me?"
- Write in your study journal questions you have, and use the scriptures, words of latter-day prophets, and other study resources to find answers.
- In the margins write scripture references that clarify the passages you are studying.
- Try writing the main idea of a passage in your words in a sentence or short paragraph.
- Look for key words and make sure you understand what they mean. Use the footnotes, Bible Dictionary, or another dictionary for definitions of unfamiliar words or phrases. Examine the surrounding words or phrases for clues to what the key words mean.
- Look for connecting words and relationships between key words and phrases. Circle key words and then draw lines to link closely related words.
- Avoid excessive marking. The benefit is lost if you cannot understand your markings because you have too many notes, lines, and colors. Underline only a few key words to highlight the verse, section, or chapter.
- Use *True to the Faith*, the Bible Dictionary, and Topical Guide as you study specific topics and doctrines.
- Use the missionary lessons, supporting scriptures, *Preach My Gospel*, and the accompanying personal study activities to guide your study.[12]

Raising the bar of knowledge of the doctrines of the gospel is vital for missionaries today as they teach by the Spirit in their own words. The more they know the gospel, the more confident and powerful will they be as teachers. So it is with our students. The more we try the virtue of the word of God by teaching doctrine—by helping them connect the dots and know how to study more effectively—the greater will be their confidence in sharing the gospel with friends, family, and others they encounter throughout their lives. Learning, loving, and living Christ's doctrine makes us better missionaries, but more important, as President Packer declared, it changes our attitudes and behaviors and thus deepens our discipleship. Because of that, we cannot be satisfied with merely getting our students *through the scriptures*. We must get the scriptures and doctrines of the gospel through *them*—deep within their minds and hearts and ever ready on the tips of their tongues. "We possess these precious truths," Elder Maxwell insightfully observed. "Now they must come to possess us!"[13]

Know *How* to Share the Gospel

During an interview with a missionary that was struggling and wanted to go home, I heard an interesting yet disturbing comment. The elder said, "I have always wanted to go on a mission. I just didn't know that I would have to talk to so many people about the gospel." I was perplexed. What did he think he would be doing as missionary? Unfortunately, this wasn't the only missionary who expressed those sentiments. There were more than a few. Another said, "I think I could be a good missionary if I didn't have to talk to people." Huh? As I scratched my head in bewilderment with this line of reasoning, it dawned on me why they would say such a thing. They had desired to serve as missionaries. They had prepared by saving money, keeping themselves worthy, and studying the scriptures. What they had not done, however, was actually talk to people (particularly those not of our faith) about the gospel. They had *prepared* but hadn't really taken the opportunity to *practice* by actually doing what missionaries do. Talking about and desiring to do missionary work is the easy part. Doing it, however, is the hard part. If you don't think so, ask almost any member about their personal member-missionary efforts. Part of the all-too-common condition I call "member-missionary paralysis" comes from not knowing *how* to share the gospel with others and an inability to recognize the abundant opportunities all around us to do so.

"The single most important thing you can do to prepare for a call to serve [as a full-time missionary] is to *become* a missionary long before you *go* on a mission" Elder David A. Bednar taught. "You will not suddenly or magically be transformed into a prepared and obedient missionary on the day you walk through the front door of the Missionary Training Center. . . . Thus, a key element of raising the bar includes working to become a missionary before going on a mission."[14] It was not surprising to me as a mission president that those young men and women who had experiences in talking about the gospel with nonmember friends or family members were much more confident in the mission field. Many came from areas where there were few Latter-day Saints in their schools and neighborhoods. Yet others came from predominantly Latter-day Saint communities. It was apparent from them that *being* a missionary—having experiences in sharing the gospel with others—was not so much a matter of geography as it was a deep love for the gospel, a recognition of its fruits in their lives, and a willingness to share personal feelings about those things. These things can and should exist in the lives of our students wherever they reside—whether they are the only Latter-day Saint in their school or whether there are no Latter-day Saints. What can we, as religious educators, do to foster those feelings and give prospective missionaries greater skills in teaching about their beliefs and sharing their testimonies of the gospel?

"Teach One Another the Doctrine of the Kingdom"

Zone conferences, district meetings, and companionship study in the mission field are filled with settings whereby missionaries teach each other and then practice important skills. While I am not equating our seminary, institute, and religion classes with zone conference, I do see a parallel. Since coming home from my mission, I have realized that I can involve my students more in teaching each other the doctrines of the kingdom as the Lord commanded in D&C 88:77. There are many ways whereby we can do that. It could take the form of having our students teach a substantial portion of a lesson, small discussion groups, role plays, and individual responses to the simple question, How would you explain that to someone not of our faith? There is a temptation to be the dispenser of information rather than a director of learning. Undoubtedly, we learn more when we have to teach others. As a result, our students—prospective full-time missionaries and future moms and dads in "gospel-sharing homes"[15]—will be better prepared to share their testimonies and discuss their beliefs if they don't just sit in our classes and soak it up but rather share with others what they have soaked up.

All too often, I think that there is good participation in my classes if I have students read a few scriptures or answer some shallow question that requires a no-brainer response. Now as I more conscientiously seek to afford my students opportunities to teach one another, I try to envision real-life situations that missionaries and members constantly encounter necessitating clear, concise, and convincing explanations. For example, I could pose this challenge to my students: "Tell me about the Book of Mormon—what it is, how we got it, and how you feel about it—in two minutes." There are numerous ways whereby we can get our students to teach one another and address real-life missionary challenges. My students usually have more relevant situations, including questions they have been asked or challenges to our beliefs they have encountered. Those are often great teaching and missionary-preparing moments. Likewise, now when teaching a scripture block, instead of just calling on a student to read, I ask my students to look at the context of the passage and then explain in their own words what is being taught. Similarly, when we have discussed doctrinal concepts, I invite students to summarize (usually in a minute or less) what we discussed in such a way that one who had not been involved in the entire class would understand the doctrine. Being able to synthesize and summarize, both verbally and in writing, is vital to acquiring greater doctrinal knowledge and valuable in sharing the gospel with others.

Several years ago when I served in a stake presidency, the stake president gave an assignment to the stake council and bishoprics. We were to write a summary of the entire plan of salvation that could be read in less than two minutes. At each meeting thereafter for many months we read to each other our short summaries of the plan. It was difficult to do, but enlightening. I learned a great deal from the insights of others. Perhaps you should try it. Such a doctrinal synthesis paper could be done on any variety of gospel principles. A colleague once said, "You don't really know what you believe until you have to write it so clearly that no one could misunderstand." That is why missionaries are instructed to write lesson plans or outlines each time they teach. As religious educators, we do the same thing. Perhaps we should give our students an opportunity to do the same. The more opportunities we can provide for our students to learn how to teach and talk about the gospel in a clear and concise manner, the more prepared and confident they will be to share the gospel with others.

"Stand as Witnesses of God at All Times"

As much as I love missionary work and preparing future missionaries, I am personally uncomfortable giving my students assignments to share the gospel with their friends of other faiths. To me, missionary work is not a project. I hope my students are praying for and having missionary experiences. I hope those preparing to serve full-time missions go with the missionaries to teaching appointments as directed and approved by local leaders. As a religious educator, I can't control that. What I can do, however, is to keep in the forefront of my teaching the tremendous blessings we have by reason of the restored gospel, the privilege of being members of the Church, and the covenantal responsibilities we took with baptism. I can teach that in every volume of scripture we are reminded that through our efforts as the seed of Abraham "shall all the families of the earth be blessed, even with the blessings of the Gospel, which are the blessing of salvation, even of life eternal" (Abraham 2:11). I can teach and testify that missionary work is directly linked to the Atonement of Christ. The more I feel the love of the Savior in my life, the greater is my desire to stand as a witness of the Lord and share what He has done for me with others around me. In fact, sharing the gospel with others is a manifestation of our love for the Savior and our gratitude for His sacrifice in our behalf. President Howard W. Hunter declared, "Any time we experience the blessings of the Atonement in our lives, we cannot help but have a concern for the welfare of others. . . . A great indicator of one's personal conversion is the desire to share the gospel with others."[16] The more we can help our students understand *who* they are, *what* the Atonement has done for them, and *why* the Lord expects them to share the gospel with others, the *how* of missionary work becomes clearer. As President Henry B. Eyring taught:

> I've studied carefully and prayerfully some who are remarkably faithful and effective witnesses of the Savior and His Church. Their stories are inspiring. . . .
>
> There is no single pattern in what they do. There is no common technique. . . . They each seem to get a different answer, suited especially to them and to the people they meet.
>
> But in one way they are all alike. It is this: they have a common way of seeing who they are. They can do what they have been inspired to do because of who they are. To do what we are to do, we will have to become like them in at least two ways. First, they feel they are the beloved children of a loving Heavenly Father. Because of that, they turn to Him easily and often in prayer. They expect to receive His personal direction. They obey in meekness and humility, like the children of a perfect parent. He is close to them.
>
> Second, they are the grateful disciples of the resurrected Jesus Christ. They know for themselves that the Atonement is real and necessary for all. They have felt cleansed through baptism by those in authority and the receipt of the Holy Ghost for themselves. . . .

> Those who speak easily and often of the restored gospel prize what it has meant to them. They think of that great blessing often. It is the memory of the gift they have received which makes them eager for others to receive it. They have felt the love of the Savior.[17]

Conclusion

Being a mission president was for me the most intense, most busy, most demanding, most difficult, most tiring—both physically and emotionally—and most rewarding thing, outside of my family, I have ever done in my life. What a privilege it was to serve! I don't know whether I did any good for others, but I know the mission did good for me. I am different because of it and I will be forever grateful for that transformation. I am often asked, "What do you miss the most from your mission?" Like any returning missionary, young or old, there are many things that will be deeply missed. (There are also many things that I won't miss!) I already miss the constant involvement with the full-time missionaries—the teaching, training, encouraging, and lifting. I miss seeing the miracles that occurred within them and the miracles they wrought around them.

Upon returning to my faculty position at BYU, I must admit that I was disappointed that I was not assigned to teach Religion 130, sharing the gospel. But now I realize that all that I teach—whatever the course, whatever the concept—is truly missionary preparation and sharing the gospel. All of our students—and all of us, as well—are part of the prophetically envisioned "greatest generation of missionaries in the history of the Church." For that vision to be realized, we must be the greatest generation of religious educators—missionary preparers, testimony strengtheners, gospel scholar developers, doctrinal dot-connectors, and by all means, faith builders. That is a lot to do. That is a serious and sacred responsibility. So as my missionaries would often say, "Let's step up. There's a bar that needs raising."

Notes

1. M. Russell Ballard, in Conference Report, October 2002, 50.
2. Ballard, in Conference Report, October 2002, 52; emphasis added.
3. Ballard, in Conference Report, October 2002, 57.
4. James E. Faust, in Conference Report, April 1996, 59.

5. Neal A. Maxwell, "The Inexhaustible Gospel," in *1991–92 Speeches* (Provo, UT: Brigham Young University), 141.
6. William R. Bradford, in Conference Report, October 1987, 90.
7. Harold B. Lee, "President Harold B. Lee Directs Church; Led by the Spirit," *Church News*, July 15, 1972, 4.
8. Boyd K. Packer, in Conference Report, October 1986, 20.
9. "Statement on Missionary Work," First Presidency letter, December 11, 2002.
10. *Preach My Gospel* (Salt Lake City: The Church of Jesus Christ of Latter-day Saints, 2004), 21.
11. *Preach My Gospel*, 29.
12. These study suggestions are adapted from *Preach My Gospel*, 22–24.
13. Neal A. Maxwell, in Conference Report, April 1986, 45.
14. David A. Bednar, in Conference Report, October 2005, 47–48.
15. See M. Russell Ballard, in Conference Report, April 2006, 88.
16. Howard W. Hunter, "The Atonement and Missionary Work," seminar for new mission presidents, June 1994, quoted in *Preach My Gospel*, 13.
17. Henry B. Eyring, in Conference Report, April 2003, 30–31.

Helping Children to Be Lifelong Learners

Don and Ann Pearson

Don and Ann Pearson *are the parents of six children and live in Glendale, California. Both graduated from BYU, and Don then received his law degree from Harvard University.*

When our oldest son, Eric, was four, I was reading him a picture book, *Paddy Pork and His Ballooning Adventures*. I told the story from the pictures: "Paddy Pork is in a hot air balloon. He is landing on that island. He is dropping a line over the side of the balloon."

Eric stopped me. "That's not a line; it's a rope."

I looked at Eric and then back at the book and continued. "He is getting out of the balloon and trying to climb down the tree. Oh no, his coat is caught on a limb."

Eric said, "That's not a coat; it's a jacket."

I was somewhat annoyed and said, "Eric, there are no words in this book—only pictures. How can you tell that that is a rope and not a line and a jacket and not a coat? I am a lawyer and went to law school and now get paid a lot of money to make careful distinctions, and I can't tell, so how do you know?"

He thought for a long time and then said, "Mother told me." Of course, she had read the book to him probably a hundred times by then.

"Do you think your mother is the final authority in this house?" I asked.

His little lip quivered, and he carefully thought before answering, "No, you are."

My chest expanded with this exceptional answer, but then, like the lawyer on cross-examination who asked one question too many, I asked, "How did you know that?"

He responded, "Mother told me."

Although somewhat humbling, this experience caused me to reflect on the principle in the proclamation on the family that states "fathers and mothers are obligated to help one another as *equal* partners."[1]

At the request of the *Religious Educator*, we have attempted to share some of what we have learned as parents and to outline some of our thoughts about education. The stories, experiences, and insights in this essay are our stories and experiences with our six children and are put together in an effort to give ideas that have worked for us. Most of the ideas are not groundbreaking, but they illustrate that "by small and simple things are great things brought to pass" (Alma 37:6).

Each of our six children has served a full-time mission, and each has graduated from college and has completed an advanced degree, except our youngest, Steven, who completed his undergraduate degree from BYU in April of 2007 and is currently planning to enter an MBA program. Sometimes people ask us, "How did you get your kids to do well in school?" The short answer is that we have been blessed with remarkable children. The long answer is (l) we loved learning and tried to be examples to our children of that love, (2) we read with our children and encouraged them in their reading, (3) we found opportunities for teaching and learning in day-to-day activities, (4) we were actively involved in discussions and decisions about education at every level of their schooling, and (5) we had dinner together as a family.

General Principles

We have found many ways to make learning fun for our family, including the following:

1. *Share your love of learning.* We like to tell our children the story about how we met as college students. Ann and I met in a New Testament class at Brigham Young University. Before the semester ended, we were studying together the great themes of the four Gospels. At the end of the semester, in preparation for the final exam, we enjoyed reviewing class notes together and creating outlines and memorizing key scriptures on baptism, service, and discipleship, among other themes. There was something fun about the intensity

of the learning process and in preparing for the final examination. Learning was exhilarating, and studying together made it more enjoyable.

Over the years, we hoped that our interest in books and words and ideas would be so much a part of us that it would bubble out spontaneously. Our interest in world, national, Church, and local news is a part of who we are.

2. *Spend time together.* One of the greatest joys of being a parent is doing things with your children. We felt that time should be spent in a variety of different activities as well as in various combinations with family members:

- parents and all the children together
- mother one-on-one with each child
- father one-on-one with each child
- mother and father together with each child

In the last category, we planned one major vacation with each child during his or her growing-up years. What a wonderful interpersonal and educational experience for parents and child alike!

3. *Take advantage of learning opportunities.* Although there is no substitute for school, there is also no substitute for learning when school is out. Just as Alma taught that we should pray always in our fields and in our hearts, so we should be always learning from the daily activities of which we are a part. All of life is a learning process, and there are thousands of golden moments to teach and to learn. We used dinner time, driving time, and early morning time as bonus learning times by talking about subjects of interest and importance in our children's schoolwork or scripture study.

Marianne recalls the time on the freeway when an understanding of fractions came to her. She was five or six at the time. The freeway sign said "Los Feliz—1/2 mile." We talked about what the "1" stood for, what the "2" stood for, and that for a mile with two parts, only one part was left until we came to the exit. I don't know why she learned it on the freeway; it would have been easier at the dinner table to talk about half of an orange because it would have been so much more visible than half of a mile.

When driving alone to or from work, Church, or business meetings, I listen to educational tapes or CDs, especially history and literature, or I listen to the scriptures. I recently listened to the *Lord of the Rings* trilogy. We have encouraged our children to use blocks of free time each week in meaningful ways.

The Don and Ann Pearson family

Preschool and Elementary

Although there are preschool years, there are no prelearning years. It is obvious that babies and toddlers have dramatic learning curves. In advance of walking and talking, they see everything and they hear everything, and most, or at least much, of what they see and hear is retained.

The preschool and elementary years are an immense block of time. Even assuming a mission and graduate school, they represent half or almost half of all of the learning years that comprise a formal education. They are vastly undervalued and vastly underutilized.

A child under the age of twelve should have the opportunity to explore many interests and begin to develop many skills; however, we tried to be selective so that what was done could be enjoyed and done well. We tried to see that those early years were used to the maximum advantage, bearing in mind that we wanted balanced, happy children who had time to play, work at home, be involved in Church and sports, and still have time for themselves. For us, these activities didn't include helping them find TV time or computer and electronic game time. When our older children were young, we kept our TV in a closet and brought it out only for special times.

1. *Show love.* It is easy to love a child, especially your own child, and learning is helped by love. As a mother shows or tells a child the way to do something, her love is felt by her child, and that love reinforces learning. It also affects the quality of teaching; without love, the teacher's interest in the learning process is not the same, and without love, the toddler's interest in the learning process is not the same.

2. *Encourage independence.* Each of our children learned very early how to say, "I will do it myself." Learning is doing and then doing it again—not just watching and then watching again. No child or adult ever learned to play the piano by watching. Let them do it—whatever "it" is—as soon as they can. Find opportunities for them to serve others and meet challenges successfully through their own efforts.

3. *Celebrate achievements.* The ultimate reward of learning is to have learned. But recognition from parents and others is a great motivator. Sometimes we would have a child repeat an Article of Faith or a scripture at family home evening and then present the child with a certificate for the accomplishment. "To Laura Pearson for learning the 10th Article of Faith." "To Thomas Mack Pearson for counting to 100." Presenting the certificate in a formal way at a formal meeting (family home evening) was fun. We often had the child receiving the certificate come forward and be lifted up on the table. He or she would be presented the certificate and congratulated. The award presentation would be formal and serious with shaking hands and a hug and sometimes a picture. The certificate and picture, if a picture had been taken, would then be placed on the refrigerator door.

4. *Make reading fun.* The ability to read is the foundation of all learning. The key is practice, and practice should be fun. We tried to be sure the child was practicing at the right level so that it could be fun.

We did not set out to teach our children to read before formally learning to read in school because we wanted their school experience to hold some excitement. But we did want them to be prepared to learn to read when that time came. As they asked about letters and words, we found it natural to help them learn the alphabet and the sound each letter makes. The first word a child wants to learn to recognize and write is his or her own name. As we read to our children and as they looked at cereal boxes, toys, and games, they discovered letters and then words. Group scripture reading was a time when our beginning readers took great joy in finding and marking words they recognized in their own copy of the Book of Mormon.

As we drove in the car, we would point to a sign and ask, "What is that letter?" or "What sound does that letter make?" Sometimes we played the alphabet game (finding the alphabet letters in order from A to Z on road signs). Older siblings love being on a team with a younger brother or sister who can't read but can recognize letters. Thus, words were presented as a natural part of daily living (and it helped to pass those long minutes driving older siblings to baseball practice or piano lessons).

The very most significant tool for parents in helping young children develop reading skills, prior to their being able to read themselves, is reading aloud together. Reading books is interesting and fun. Good stories are imaginative and informative. Bedtime was the most regular time for reading aloud in our family.

One night when Karen had just turned two, her older brother and sister had been permitted to spend the night at cousins, and I was helping her get ready for bed. I turned out the light and gave her a bottle. She refused the bottle and said, "Prayer, brush teeth, story!" Each child felt entitled to his or her bedtime story, and after it was read, they asked to "please read it again." And that is what we wanted them to say—we wanted them to fall in love with books. We cherished this time, free from distractions, when we could nestle together and share the wide world of life's experiences through books and the discussion they inspired.

Even well into the elementary years, each child chose a book every evening. Sometimes an older child would do the reading to a younger one, but the child always wanted a parent nearby to appreciate the reading and to be a part of that bedtime ritual.

We enjoyed reading to our children. We enjoyed listening to them read out loud to us. We enjoyed reading together by taking turns in the same chapter of scriptures or a book or short story. We read Mark Twain's *Tom Sawyer* after dinner over a period of weeks. It was fun. Karen remembers that she could hardly wait for dinner to end so we could reach the next part of *Tom Sawyer*. Reading should be fun. It should be informative. It should be exciting. Every child should have the experience of reading a book that he or she cannot put down. We tried to help our children find that book.

Before leaving elementary school, a child should be able to read well. It doesn't make any difference what else is covered in the curriculum at this level if a child comes away with inadequate reading skills. When one of our children was struggling with a skill, we made it a goal to work on it at home with charts and prizes and extra coaching. One daughter decided in the sixth grade to relearn the way she held her pencil to improve her penmanship. We rewarded her efforts, and after several months of practice, she was pleased with her new style and was comfortable in writing.

Our children enjoyed a formalized learning time at home in their preschool years and during the summer in later years. To them, it was fun. To their mother, it was easier to keep the children happy. I went by the philosophy that little children are happiest when their hands are busy and their tummies are full (the philosophy works well for teenagers and fathers too).

We were blessed to have other families nearby who felt the way we did, and the children had many group activity times in each other's homes, which made it more fun for them and alternately freed up the mothers. One summer our family and another family combined to study transportation. We read, created, wrote, and then rode as many things as we could arrange to ride.

Laura remembers spending one summer putting together her alphabet book. There was a section of the book for each letter, and in that section there were pictures and objects cut out from magazines and newspapers whose name or description started with that letter.

5. *Help children to be precise in their thinking and use of words.* We tried to help our children learn at early ages to be precise in their use of words, and to distinguish between words and meanings. When Eric was three or four, I asked him one Sunday after church, "What did you talk about in class today?" He responded, "I didn't talk about anything." When I asked him what his teacher talked about, he responded with some detail that she had talked about the blind man whom Jesus gave a blessing and healed.

Later, our hamster died. We dug a grave out in the canyon and as we walked back to the house we discussed how the spirit leaves the body when a person or animal dies. I said, "Now that the grave is ready, let's go get the hamster." Eric responded, "You mean the hamster's body."

Laura liked to talk on the telephone when she was four years old. So Ann had to explain that you could not just talk on the telephone at any time, but only when you had something really important to say. Moments later Laura was back on the phone. Ann explained that she had just been told not be to the phone unless she had something important to say. Laura said, "Mother, I was telling my friend Rena to keep the commandments!"

Learning to make careful distinctions is an important skill and can be understood by young children.

6. *Teach numbers and math concepts.* Counting is a great activity wherever you are. We counted the number of motorcycles or the number of red cars or big trucks or, as the children got older, out-of-state license plates. This activity also taught the important skill of making distinctions: What is a red car or a big truck? Where is Wyoming? These are wonderful discussions for a child about to enter school or already in school.

Concepts of addition and subtraction are also easy to develop within almost any daily situation. How many friends can you invite to our house? How many plates do we need to put on the table for dinner if everyone in our family is here? How many more if Grandmother and Grandfather come for dinner?

Following a recipe, measuring and cutting, using money, playing board games, timing a jog around the park, reading music, and participating in many more activities of daily life provided some of the meaningful and fun learning experiences in our home. And so, as with reading, understanding of math can be developed naturally. Practice can become a game, and deficiencies in ability should be met with extra help, practice, and rewards for persistence.

7. *Allow children to teach.* Our children enjoyed playing school. When school ended after Marianne's fourth-grade year, she started a summer school for neighborhood children. This school included her two younger brothers, Tom and Steven, who were ages five and three at that time. However, her students were generally ages four to six. She had a two-hour school three mornings a week for six weeks and continued this for five summers. What a powerful experience for her—not just in teaching but in organizing, disciplining, and keeping the attention of a roomful of little boys. She also had to collect what she was owed from the parents of the students attending. Ann was always in the house to oversee things, but it was Marianne's school.

Every child needs a turn to be a teacher. It opens a different vision of both teaching and learning. The direct benefits of learning what you are required to teach is obvious to all parents.

8. *Use summertime to advantage.* The summers were a wonderful time to for our children to advance at their own pace and interest. But summer charts kept them focused on their responsibilities at home (chores and household tasks) as well as on fun activities (parties, playing with friends, and sports) and

learning opportunities (reading books and scriptures and engaging in school-like study). Items on the charts were checked off for the day, week, month, or summer, and the children were rewarded for having completed them.

Our children liked this system so well that they requested summer charts well into high school, and they continue to create them for their own children today. We discovered that a significant key to their success was having them ready to go the first week school was out while the children were still used to an early-morning routine.

Junior High and High School

As the children grew older, they could tackle more difficult tasks. During grades seven through twelve, formal education became more demanding of a child's time and focus.

1. *Develop writing skills.* Eric came home in tears one day from junior high school. He had an assignment to write two pages about himself. "I don't know how to do this, and I can't do this, and that stupid teacher shouldn't ask us to write two pages about ourselves." The more he thought about it, the more miserable he became. He was unwilling to make notes or an outline of what he wanted to write.

Finally, I took out of my briefcase the dictating equipment that I use at my law office. The equipment is small and can be held in one hand. I showed Eric how to work it. Then, I said, "Now, just tell me about yourself with the 'record' button on." When he was finished, we typed it. Then, we discussed how it should be changed to say what he wanted to say. He learned that he could write something meaningful.

I don't think he (or anyone) finds writing easy, but I can't recall him saying again about a written assignment, "I just can't do that."

Some parents and students say, "Don't take that class because the teacher is so demanding. You have to write a lot of papers." Ann and I would say to our children, "That sounds like a great class. You will learn a lot." And if you have to write, you do learn a lot. There is no other way. Good writing is good thinking on paper.

We hoped that each of our children would have one or more teachers in high school who were truly fastidious about papers being grammatically correct. Spelling must be correct. Subjects and verbs must agree. Pronouns must have an antecedent. Punctuation must be correct. Poor quality in English presentation is as bad as poor analysis and makes good analysis almost impossible to see. The very best of ideas sandwiched in between poor grammar and misspelled words will likely be lost on the reader (and grader).

2. *Have high expectations.* Marianne related an experience that she had in the seventh grade. She received a C on the first test in her English class that fall. She was afraid to tell us but did so. She said that we reacted calmly (not what she was expecting), saying, "Marianne, we think you can do better than that, and we will help you." In this literature class, the assignment was to read one short story each day. Ann or I would also read the story and discuss it with Marianne. She remembers that we showed her how to make notes about each story's characters and plot. We reviewed her notes with her in preparation for the next test. She received an A on it. This experience increased her confidence and taught her a study strategy that she has used and reused since. We somewhat dropped out of seventh-grade English for most of the rest of the year, except for when something was just too interesting not to read and discuss with her.

Children almost never perform above the expectation. If a son or daughter believes a B is his or her best, it usually will be. Balancing expectation and approval of the performance given is sometimes a challenge. We have always said to a child: "If that is your very best, that is all we ask of you. We are proud of you and your hard work."

3. *Encourage wise class choices.* The question, "What classes should I take?" is asked by students every year. A high-school student who is serious about college preparation should take classes each semester in English, mathematics (including computer science classes), history, science, and foreign language. Such a schedule will prepare him or her well. Such classes help develop critical thinking skills, which ultimately is what good education is about.

There is no substitute for good English grammar and usage. History and other subjects, as well as English literature, all require careful reading, analysis, and writing in English.

There is no substitute for math. Ideally, a student will have completed in high school at least precalculus and one calculus course. For many college graduates today, the last math class they ever took was in high school. To complete high school with calculus requires a math class every semester.

In today's world, computer skills are critical and are a foundation on which communication in humanities, business, and all disciplines build. History is fun and essential to a good humanities background. Sciences should include biology, chemistry, and physics. Language has many purposes, not the least of which is to strengthen and improve English. Latin especially helps students to understand English language structure and to improve vocabulary significantly.

4. *Encourage personal discipline and study skills.* Participation in music, athletics, and early-morning seminary requires that a student learn personal discipline. High school becomes a crucial time of decision as children need to focus their time to a greater degree on the things they want to do the most. Choosing those things should be a matter of discussion and prayer.

Our daughter Karen participated in sports in high school and was active in student government and seminary. How did she do it and maintain a high level in her academic studies? She says that athletics and school and Church activities did not cause her to underperform academically. The challenge required her to focus and use her study time wisely. Athletics, music, seminary, student government, and other similar time demands need to be balanced.

It was important to be sure their schedules were not too full. Overscheduling is as bad as or perhaps even worse than underscheduling. High performance in four or five classes is better than mediocre performance in six. A high GPA is essential for good college opportunities, but it is more critical for a student's self-assessment. If a student is getting A grades and has that expectation, then that is the level to which the student performs. If a student is getting B grades but there is an A level of expectation, neither the student nor the student's parents are happy.

Sometimes in high school (as contrasted with college), taking fewer classes is not a choice. The school may require a certain number of classes and may allow one study hall but not an option of two. Then, reducing the number of honors or AP classes may be the only way of balancing the intensity.

Occasionally, other students in our stake will discuss their schedules with me, and I often find them to be intense and wonderful schedules. But when I ask if they will have sufficient study time to prepare for their classes, I find they are working fifteen hours a week and have sports or other significant extracurricular activities. It sometimes seems to me that it will be impossible for them to perform well in all of the classes they are planning to take. I do not think it is possible to perform at a high level in difficult classes with inadequate study time. It would be better to drop one or more classes and have time to prepare well for those remaining.

We are not much on study-skills classes, but we are high on study skills. It is mostly discipline, and it is a lot about *getting started in a good location*. That is why we like a free period in the library at the school.

5. *Schedule free periods of time.* Sometimes study at home is more difficult to start and more difficult to maintain. If it is late in the day after athletics, the body and mind are tired and have less focus and energy. If the school permits or requires a free period or periods during the day, that is wonderful (in college, you can design your schedule with free periods in between difficult classes). Free periods are a great opportunity to prepare for the next class or classes and to prepare for tests later in the schedule that day, as well as for a desired change of pace for the body. When well used, they permit a burst of academic energy during that hour. Students should be certain to select a study spot in the library where they can concentrate and be effective. This is not a social hour and should be one of the best study hours of the day. It can be used as preparation time or for a final test review, and it will reduce late-night studying. When advising my children, I preferred to see that free period in middle of the day's schedule where it can be truly valuable. Neither the first nor last period of the day is nearly as valuable.

6. *Prepare for the SAT/ACT.* The SAT and ACT are extremely important because they are critical to college admission decisions. They are important for a student's academic stature in high school, too. They are critical for scholarships and high-school graduation awards.

Practice is most helpful. The argument that these tests are so broad that there is nothing anyone can do to prepare is simply false. First, taking practice exams is absolutely essential to understand how the test works, what counts and does not count, or when a guess hurts or does not hurt in the overall score. Second, a good math review is substantive and can refresh skills in areas that will be tested. Practice review will not make up for algebra or geometry classes that have never been taken, but it will sharpen the knowledge of those and related subjects for the test. Practice tests will not likely strengthen vocabulary significantly, but the practice tests will help students know the format and be familiar with the types of questions and analysis to be expected. Practice applies to the PSAT too; the better the PSAT, the better the SAT will be.

We have found short one-on-one paid SAT review courses expensive but worthwhile. It helps to have someone other than the parent working with the student and moving the SAT review forward. Having a schedule is an important benefit, as is having someone working with the subject material and with other students in preparation for the exam on a regular basis.

7. *Take advanced placement classes and exams.* It gives great freedom to a college schedule to have a number of credits from advanced placement. Students should not hesitate to challenge exams for which they think they are qualified but haven't taken the advanced-placement class. Sample questions from past tests and study books are available to help with challenge decisions. Laura studied music theory as a part of her ten years of piano lessons and state certification program. With some additional review prepared by her piano teacher, she was able to pass the music theory exam. Steven chose to prepare for an advanced-placement exam as a part of an independent study class during his senior year.

8. *Use materials outside of high school.* Steven was required to have credit in art to graduate but didn't want to give up an academic period to take the class. Instead, during the summer before starting twelfth grade, he took Art History 101 online for credit from BYU. He received college credit, and the class was accepted for his high-school graduation requirement. BYU has many outstanding online classes, both at the high-school and college levels. They are worth considering, especially in the summer.

Students should be able to get an A in an online class, as they can retake the quizzes and sometimes the exams for a fee. Our only rule for the children was that they must have completed the online class they were taking before starting another online class.

9. *Use summers meaningfully.* During their high-school years, we hoped our children would have a unique educational or work experience during the summers. Fortunately, we didn't find it necessary to use summers to catch up on core academic subjects. After seventh, eighth, and ninth grades, they occasionally used summer classes to accelerate in math or language. Good work opportunities in our community are limited for their age. Tom and Steven both took Algebra II in summer school, which permitted them to start pre-calculus a year earlier and take additional math and computer classes before they graduated. Because of earlier language background, Steven took Spanish 2 one summer, which permitted him to start Spanish 3 in the ninth grade. He spent the summer after ninth grade living and going to school in Chile. This experience made a huge difference in his Spanish conversation skills.

Laura and Marianne were exchange students with American Field Service, Laura in Turkey and Marianne in Argentina. These were interesting and very broadening experiences. Perhaps we are too protective, but there were aspects of their experiences that were a little frightening. Steven's experience in Chile, where he lived in two different Latter-day Saint homes, was much more comfortable for us. Karen did a "People to People" exchange tour program in Russia and Scandinavia. Living in a foreign country was a great experience for each of our children, and created a wonderful, powerful appreciation of the United States of America.

10. *Teach children to make good choices.* Great scholastic training without good common sense still leaves us short in life's journey. We tried to involve our children, when appropriate, in helping us exercise good judgment as parents and also to trust in their judgment. One of a high-school student's most significant decisions is which college to attend. We encouraged our children to consider applying to several schools. We discussed with them questions concerning these choices, such as "Where will you receive the best educational training?" "Where will you meet the most friends and form lasting, lifelong friendships?" "Where will you enjoy college the most?"

One of our trips was a BYU Travel Study tour of Mexico and Guatemala with our middle daughter, Karen. One evening we went out to eat at a restaurant in Guatemala City. We had been seated, and we ordered. Immediately after ordering, Karen said she was impressed that we should not stay at that restaurant. We called the waiter and apologized that we were canceling our order and would need to leave. Neither of us remembered this incident in detail, and when Karen told this story recently, we asked her what happened. She responded, "I don't know what happened at the restaurant or what would have happened to us had we stayed, but I will forever remember that my parents would act on my impression alone. You said, 'Karen, we don't have those same impressions, but if you have an impression that we should leave, then we should leave.'"

Conclusion

We can summarize our strategies very succinctly: Love learning. Do things together and use learning opportunities in day-to-day activities. Focus on basic reading skills. Finally, be involved in the classroom content with your son or daughter, not just the extracurricular activities. By getting involved in everyday learning activities, parents will have some great experiences with their children and will set them on the course to becoming lifelong learners.

Note

1. "The Family: A Proclamation to the World," *Ensign*, November 1995, 102; emphasis added.

As part of an active learning experience, student Natalie Manwaring creates an audio version of an article for the Religious Studies Center Web site.

On Getting Engaged

Kathy Kipp Clayton

Kathy Kipp Clayton *is a member of the Religious Studies Center advisory board.*

I did not grow up with the gospel in my home, but because of a teacher I had as a young woman, I gained a personal testimony of the reality of my Savior's love. My teacher did not live within my ward boundaries, nor did I ever attend her formal classes, but I claim her nonetheless. My teacher was a regular on the Church-speaking circuit, and she invited me to be her visual aid. After she had offered extensive, important instruction to her congregation, she invited me to sing "I Know That My Redeemer Lives" as an illustration of the principles she had taught. I was flattered to be invited, and I sang with my whole heart to please and honor my mentor, but something else happened in the process. As I sang those lyrics, I knew. I knew what I was singing was true. I knew He really did live and love me "to the end." I knew that He really was "my kind, wise heav'nly Friend."[1] I knew. As I committed my voice to that task and offered the best of my young talent, heaven burned into my soul the reality of the things about which I was singing.

At new student orientation at BYU that year, an energetic presenter began by telling the freshmen that there were many myths at BYU. She assured them that some of them are true, including that students get engaged a lot. "In fact," she continued, "I have been engaged several times. I make it a goal to get engaged at least five times per semester." The new freshmen were wide eyed and giggling. She continued, "I suggest that you call your parents at the end of the semester, even at the end of this class, to tell them that you got engaged." Marriage was not the topic. Engagement in learning was. My serving as a visual aid was not critical to the success of my teacher's presentation, but being engaged in learning was critical to achieving a changed heart.

The goal of authentic student engagement might be illustrated by a lesson about an apple. A teacher who wanted her students to learn about an apple could simply stand before them and offer a well-researched, carefully prepared presentation documenting the characteristics of an apple. Likely, her students would leave the lesson with more information than they had arrived with. She could also show a picture of an apple. Those students would certainly know more still for having engaged themselves visually with the subject. The teacher might increase the breadth of the sensory connection by actually taking an apple to class for the students to see, feel, smell, and touch. But best of all, the teacher who expects to make a lasting impression on her students could take an apple to class—maybe several different types of apples—and offer tastes of them all. Those fully engaged students would leave the classroom knowing the subject personally because they had been invited to make it their own.

Psychological research demonstrates that people are more likely to "behave" their way into thinking than they are to "think" their way into behaving. Put simply, if we smile, we will actually be happier; if we whistle a happy tune, we will be less afraid; and if we count our blessings, we will feel greater gratitude. Or, as the Prophet Joseph Smith taught, "Faith is a principle of action."[2] We receive a testimony of truth and grow in faith as we live the gospel. Learning and becoming happen best by doing because "if any man will do his will, he shall know of the doctrine" (John 7:17). I sang "I Know That My Redeemer Lives," and as I sang those lyrics their truthfulness became my personal testimony. The message became my own as I did something with it. The doing afforded the Spirit the occasion to seal it upon my heart and promoted my knowing and remembering.

One thoughtful teacher who encouraged student engagement understood the difference between the impact of passive and active classroom environments. She planned her classrooms to be student workshops more than teacher presentations. To acquaint her eleven-year-old students with the priesthood, rather than lecturing those potentially restless young men on the duties and importance of the ordination they were about to receive, she escorted them to the empty baptismal font and invited them to step into that promising place and read the scriptures containing the baptismal covenant.

Together they recalled the details of their own baptisms. From there, the engaged group went to the sacrament table, where they read and discussed the scriptures relevant to the sacrament, including the sacrament prayers. They paraded to the bishop's office, where they each obtained a donation slip and proceeded to fill it out. They discussed together the importance of those donations and how they are used to help the needy. They concluded the activity with two missionaries sharing stories of spiritual experiences from their service. The eleven-year-olds were allowed to ask questions as well as handle the elders' daily planners, *Preach My Gospel* manuals, and name tags. By the end of the participatory lesson, those young men understood the priesthood more deeply and personally because they had been engaged in places and practices relative to the priesthood in an active, multisensory way.

Interactive games can be satisfying, effective ways to engage students in learning. The age-old Cub Scout acronym, KISMIF (Keep It Simple, Make It Fun), remains a valuable guideline. *The Big Book of Team Building Games* by John Newstrom and Edward Scannell thoughtfully suggests that classroom games are useful to make a clear, memorable point; build class morale; encourage trust among class members as they share insights and develop common solutions; promote flexibility among class members; and reinforce appropriate behaviors such as cooperation, listening, and creativity. Games are also inexpensive, participative, and low risk. One teacher found that a game of "Getting to Know You Bingo" on one of the first days of early-morning seminary in a class that included students from five different high schools established common ground and built bridges between students who lacked immediate connection. A connection was made between two students who were both scuba certified—one student was a young woman from the high school located just through the parking lot. The other was a hearing-impaired young man from a magnet school several blocks away. They were both made aware of something they had in common rather than believing they were very different.

At a stake girls' camp, young women from five wards were bound together in playful cooperation as they worked together to untie the human knot they had made by joining hands in a tangled fashion across a circle. They talked and strategized, then ducked under, climbed over, and twisted around in a low-risk effort to create an untangled circle. In the process, they learned important but gentle lessons about cooperation, communication, trial and error, and sticking to a task. They also gained an appreciation for the varied talents and insights of girls with whom they had not previously been acquainted. That simple, no-cost game provided a quick, playful, interactive way to encourage relationships among those girls without sitting them down for a heavy-handed lecture on the subject.

Although games have broad and compelling usefulness, several potential danger zones are important to remember. Be well prepared with all requisite props, manage time carefully, choose games that forward and fortify learning without becoming an end unto themselves, and avoid simplistic images that can be distracting, especially from sacred themes. For example, occasionally leaders invite young people to prepare extemporaneous skits using gospel themes. When the youth respond with silly presentations about sacred subjects like morality or prayer, the skits can quickly become irreverent.

Engaged learning adapts well to students' short attention span. One very able but very frustrated new Sunday School teacher returned from his first Sunday in a new class of lively adolescents ready to make an appointment with the bishop to request his release. In spite of the teacher's extensive preparation, those spirited young people had checked out barely moments into the teacher's presentation. Eager to redeem himself, that faithful teacher returned the next week with a fresh pacing strategy. He prepared his lessons in ten-minute segments titled "Into, Through, and Beyond." The "Into" section consisted of an attention-getting activity that might be as simple as a drawing, an object, a thought-provoking question, or a quick quiz. The "Through" section moved the students from that initial attention-getting activity to the concepts he sought to teach. That section might include carefully selected scripture reading, storytelling, or a comprehensible presentation of a doctrinal point. The final "Beyond" section included the all-important answer to the age-old question of teenagers, "So what?" During that segment, the teacher helped the students apply the principle to their own lives. Sometimes he began that important process by sharing a story from his personal life. Occasionally he tossed a beanbag and asked, "So what?" to the student who caught it. Always he asked carefully prepared, nonthreatening, open-ended questions to encourage thought and personal application. In the course of a thirty-minute lesson, the teacher generally moved through the cycle of "Into, Through, and Beyond" three times.

An engaged community of learners includes celebration—celebration of each other, celebration of the subject matter, and celebration of learning itself. Unfortunately, we often segregate work and play as if they were mutually exclusive, when, in reality, engaging work in the form of learning is among the most satisfying forms of play. In his book *Happier*, Tal Ben-Shahar suggests that a skillful teacher can "create environments at home and school that are conducive to the experience of present and future benefit, pleasure and meaning."[3] Especially as we engage in earnest study of the gospel, the essence of which is aptly called, the "plan of happiness," our students should find happiness, satisfaction, and even fun.

One bright and fun-loving early-morning seminary teacher organized an annual "Granny Awards" every spring, correspondent to the "Grammy Awards." For several months before the celebration, she served her family pancakes and waffles daily, smothered with Mrs. Butterworth's syrup, then saved the empty granny-shaped bottles to paint gold and use as clever awards at her seminary celebration. Students nominated characters from the volume of scripture they had been studying that year, then presented to the class their reasons why that scriptural character deserved to be awarded the "Granny" for "Best Leading Lady/Man," or "Best Supporting Lady/Man," or which scriptural story deserved the prize for "Best Overall" or "Best Story." The class voted to identify the winners, after which the student who had made the nomination accepted the golden syrup bottle. The annual celebration served as a review, involved restless students, and promoted a community of learning.

Active learning also addresses the needs of students with various learning styles. As a hopeless left-brainer, a classic linear thinker, I like lectures and find pleasure in worksheets. School in its traditional, rote rigidity is a perfect fit for me. Desks in neat rows and binders with exacting subject divisions please me. Increasingly, however, our classrooms are filled with students who learn differently. Efforts to engage students with creative and diverse strategies are essential for the nonlinear learners and refreshing for all the rest.

One Jewish convert to the Church delighted his students by providing them with an authentic Passover feast to familiarize them with the symbols of that event. Those students had a multisensory experience with bitter herbs that enabled them to understand and literally taste something of bitterness.

Another teacher appealed to the learning style of her class by creating simple rhymes and musical phrases for each of the scripture mastery verses. Those students will forever know where to find the story of Joseph fleeing from temptation. Who could forget "Genesis 39, Potiphar's wife's dirty mind"?

Students who are especially physical learners came to life in a seminary class when their teacher invited them to come to the whiteboard in groups of six until all had had a turn. After having read a scriptural passage, they were asked to write a single word or phrase in response to a question, such as "What quality do you admire about the character?" or "What is an important theme of that passage?" or "What do you appreciate about your dad/mom/bishop?" When the entire board was filled, the class read and discussed the results of their combined effort.

An unforgettable Sunday School teacher extended himself beyond the normal bounds of a formal presentation with imaginative, unpredictable "Into" activities. To familiarize the class with the elements of Daniel's dream, he brought into the Relief Society room a giant Michelin Man with all the bulgy body parts labeled to represent the various kingdoms that would be destroyed by the stone cut out of the mountain without hands. On another Sunday, class began when a noisy kazoo player began to march down the aisle blaring a raucous tune on his annoying instrument. The teacher engaged the musician in an interview to learn that he was off to pay his tithing and wanted to be sure he received appropriate credit for his good works. After that engaging "Into" activity, the class turned to Matthew for the "Through" part, a discussion of doing alms to be seen of men.

Csikszentmihalyi, in his book, *Finding Flow: The Psychology of Engagement With Everyday Life*, writes: "Neither parents nor schools are very effective at teaching the young to find pleasure in the right things. Adults, themselves often deluded by infatuation with fatuous models, conspire in the deception. They make serious tasks seem dull and hard, and frivolous ones exciting and easy. Schools generally fail to teach how exciting, how mesmerizingly beautiful science or mathematics can be; they teach the routine of literature or history rather than the adventure."[4]

How much more "mesmerizingly beautiful" is the gospel than even the best of science or mathematics! With creative engagement, students can taste the delicious fruits of active learning—sometimes even literally. Faith is a principle of action. As teachers facilitate classrooms that promote authentic, active student engagement, students will find learning as delicious as a ripe apple, as memorable as a favorite song, and as personal as a visit to the baptismal font. They will "behave" their way into "knowing" and get happily engaged again and again.

Notes

1. "I Know That My Redeemer Lives," *Hymns* (Salt Lake City: The Church of Jesus Christ of Latter-day Saints, 1985), no. 136.
2. Joseph Smith, *Lectures on Faith: Delivered to the School of the Prophets in Kirtland, Ohio, 1834–35* (Salt Lake City: Deseret Book, 1985), 1:9.
3. Tal Ben-Shahar, *Happier* (New York: McGraw-Hill, 2007), 86.
4. Mihaly Csikszentmihalyi, quoted in Ben-Shahar, *Happier*, 94.

As teachers, we sometimes get pulled into a contest of wills with a student, and it becomes difficult for us to see our own contribution to the contention that exists between us.

"Tap Lightly": Managing Classroom Behavior

William C. Ostenson

William C. Ostenson *is a retired Church Educational System principal in Idaho Falls.*

Mike Mansfield, a highly respected United States senator from Montana, served as majority leader for sixteen years and, after retiring from the Senate, as an ambassador to Japan for an additional twelve years. Much of his success as a senator and an ambassador can be attributed to the fact that in his relationships with people, he always tried to "tap lightly." He picked up this saying from his nine years in the copper mines of Butte, Montana, following his service in all three branches of the military during and after World War I.

The statement came as a warning to those who used explosives to loosen the rock in which the copper ore was embedded. An experienced miner would drill holes into the rock and then place an explosive charge deep into each hole. The charges had to fit tightly deep in the rock or the force of the explosion would cause a rockslide that would almost certainly lead to sudden death. This process required the miner to tap the explosive into the hole until it reached the far end. Of course, if he tapped too hard, the charge would go off prematurely, leading to the caution, "Tap 'er light." Mike Mansfield saw in this a metaphor for dealing with people. As he sought to apply this rule in his relationships with people, he won the respect not only of Republicans and Democrats in the Senate but also of the Japanese people.[1]

Teachers and principals in the seminary program can use this same principle to solve disciplinary problems.

As a principal, I once worked with a student whose teacher had kicked him out of class for persistent disobedience. I do not recall all the complaints the teacher had about this student, but on that particular day the student had brought a can of pop into class and had refused to put it away. I invited the student into my office, and I began by getting better acquainted with him. That is not what students usually expect when going into a principal's office for disciplinary reasons; but to be of any help to this student, I needed to know something about him. Furthermore, such an approach is usually disarming, and I could address the issue at hand more easily once the student's defenses had been loosened up. After getting better acquainted, I asked him to tell me his side of the story. I find that this approach too can be disarming and can reveal a great deal about a student. "Tapping lightly" in this way is often the first step toward a solution.

When I asked the student for his side of the story, he complained that because his high-school teachers allowed him to bring pop into their classes, he couldn't see what was wrong with bringing it into seminary. I explained that this was merely the rule we had throughout the seminary, and because he was able to drink pop in all his other classes, he certainly did not *need* to drink pop in seminary. That was my way of showing my support for the teacher in that situation, and he was hard pressed to disagree. I also thought that he would agree to being more cooperative if I promised to ask his teacher to cut him some slack. He agreed to that as well, and then the teacher and I had a talk.

As teachers, we sometimes get pulled into a contest of wills with a student, and it becomes difficult for us to see our own contribution to the contention that exists between us. I could have moved this student to another class, but it seemed important that the student and teacher work through their differences. First, the young man needed to stop showing his independence through disobedience, and second, the teacher needed to learn how to tap more lightly and take it less personally when his students tested his authority.

Having worked for fourteen years as a coordinator in the U.S. Northeast Area, I knew that this young man was one of the reasons why we have released-time seminary. During my fourteen years of service to the wards and branches of northern Indiana and the northwest corner of Ohio, I had the opportunity to watch many excellent teachers teach in early-morning and home-study classes. All of them were volunteers. But the percentage of enrollment in early-morning or home-study was never as high as in released-time, which is why we rarely saw a casual student—like the young man—in those classes. Such students do come to our released-time classes, however, and as such they provide some of the justification for paying a professional teacher to teach those classes. We ought not to be too quick to dismiss them when they become a challenge for us.

As part of my assignment as a coordinator, I taught a monthly lesson to the home-study and early-morning students prior to their monthly stake, or Super Saturday, activities. I always enjoyed those classes, and I seldom had problems with discipline. Yet on one occasion the students came to class so excited that early into the lesson I had to stop and wait quietly for them to settle down. All seventy to eighty students responded to this approach except for one young lady in the very center of the chapel who resumed talking to a young man on her left as soon as I started the lesson again. When I saw her talking again, I stopped and announced that I would wait until she was finished before I continued. Having been singled out, she stomped out of the chapel, pushing her way past the students who sat between her and the aisle. I could not tell how anyone else felt, but when she got up to walk out of the room, I felt as if the Spirit walked out too.

We always held an in-service meeting for the teachers after the students left for their activity. During the meeting, I asked which teacher had that young lady in his or her local class. When I found out, I asked her teacher to do everything she could to get that young lady back again next month. I also admitted to the teachers that I had not set a very good example for how to handle a disciplinary problem, though the teachers admitted they were hard-pressed to think of another way of handling it.

For the next monthly lesson, we met in a different building, and we were in a different room than the chapel. Eighth-graders had also been invited so they could see what a Super Saturday was like because they would be attending the following year. The room was so full of people that a number of students had to sit on the floor in the front of the class. When I started the lesson, everyone was once again excited and inattentive. But I knew that I had a good lesson prepared, so I began by directing a series of questions to a group of eighth-graders sitting on the floor to my immediate right. When I saw the fear in their eyes turn into sincere interest in the lesson, I turned to another group and endeavored to pull them into the lesson as well. I kept doing that until I had everyone in the room engaged in the lesson except for the young lady from the previous month. She was sitting in the very center of the room and seemed intent on challenging my authority once again. But it was a good lesson, and she quickly became interested when I began involving her in it.

With twenty minutes left in the lesson, I saw one of our home-study teachers and another student come into the room and sit down on the floor to my left. Then I saw that teacher get up and leave, only to return moments later with another student. I was interested in what he had to say in our in-service meeting once the lesson had concluded and the students had left for their activity. First, he apologized for being late. He was a new teacher, and he had no idea how long it would take him to pick up his students who needed a ride. When they finally got there, it was so late that he could only convince one of them to come into class with him. But once he got into the room, he felt the Spirit so strongly that he left to try and convince his other students to come into the room so they could at least feel the Spirit that was there. That Saturday our in-service lesson was on how to discipline students by using questions to pull them into the lesson rather than pushing them away by pointing out their misbehavior. In other words, how do we "tap lightly" enough to loosen sometimes rock-solid resistance without having our efforts blow up in our faces?

There is no substitute for a well-prepared lesson when it comes to discipline in the classroom—and especially when it comes to those disciplinary problems that arise from boredom. Because of four years of good lessons from a variety of teachers, the young man who had brought pop into class did feel the Spirit at times and did learn some things about the gospel in spite of himself. I know that because I kept an eye on him for the next four years. And even though he did not graduate from seminary, I believe that what President Henry B. Eyring said in 1993 applied to him: "If you treat them as seekers, they will feel that you love them, and that may awaken a hope in them that they could have a softer heart. It may not happen every time, and it may not last. But it will happen often, and sometimes it will last. And all of them will at least remember that you believed in the best in them—their inheritance as a child of God."[2]

Nevertheless, part of loving and believing in them is to discipline them when they need to be disciplined. For example, when I became principal for the third time, I discovered that we had more than twenty seniors who were using their released-time status to do whatever they wanted. I had each of these students into my office to visit with them individually about their plans for the future and to ask if they were planning to graduate from seminary. All of them said they wanted to graduate, so I told them that they could as long as they never skipped class again. But if they did skip again, I would be required to dismiss them from seminary, and they would not graduate. I explained to them why it was important for them to honor their released-time contract with the high school and how important it was for us to protect our legal status as a released-time program and maintain a good relationship with the high school. I said that what I was saying had nothing to do with how I felt about them personally, as I had to live by the same rules as they did. Finally, I said that I would be calling their parents to tell them the same.

With one exception, the parents were supportive. One father said that it was about time his son was held accountable and that his son would complete his makeup work before spring break or be left home while his friends went on a trip to Lake Powell. All those students but one stopped skipping class and graduated. The one who skipped class had her enrollment discontinued, after which she came and asked if there was any way she could still graduate. Having acted blatantly in her most recent absence, I told her that I was unable to trust her enough to allow her back into released-time, but I would set up a demanding alternative for her, which, upon completion, would enable her to graduate. She accepted and graduated with her friends.

I believe the rules we have in seminary should be used to motivate our students to do what they already know they should do. In other words, we ought to always "tap lightly" with the rules rather than use them to their full weight. I have learned that if you are kind but firm with students, they almost always step up and do the right thing. When they do not, the consequences belong totally to them. We can take comfort in knowing that we have followed the admonition of President Howard W. Hunter, who encouraged us to "give a soft answer" when we might otherwise be tempted to give a harsh answer, to "encourage [our] youth" rather than discourage them, to "try to understand" them rather than being quick to judge them as lacking in spirituality or maturity, to "examine [our] demands on [them]," and to be "kind" and "gentle" with them.[3] That is good counsel for those of us who want to "tap 'er light."

Notes

1. Don Oberdorfer, *Senator Mansfield: The Extraordinary Life of a Great American Statesman and Diplomat* (Washington, DC: Smithsonian Books, 2003), 1–14.

2. Henry B. Eyring, *To Draw Closer to God: A Collection of Discourses* (Salt Lake City: Deseret Book, 1997), 146.
3. Howard W. Hunter, "This Christmas. . . ." in *LDS Church News*, December 10, 1994.

Index

Entries for images are indicated by italicized page numbers.

A

Abraham, 36–37
achievements, celebrating, 149
actions, learning through, 162
ACT test, 156–57
Adatto, Kiku, 79
analytical questions, 115–16
AP classes, 157
apple, 162
application questions, 116–17
Articles of Church, 95–96
assumptions, 132–33
Atonement: Boyd K. Packer on learning about, 6; using wake-up call when teaching, 29–30; understanding Fall as groundwork for teaching, 30–32; using Book of Mormon to teach, 32–34; using questions to teach, 34–36; using loving relationships to teach, 36–37; pure doctrine of, 37–41; teaching, compared to seed, 41–42; sharing gospel and, 141–43
awards, 149, 165

B

Ballard, Russell M.: on raising bar for missionaries, 128; on learning from teaching, 137
Banner, James, 50
baptism, teaching, 162–63
Barden, Jerusha, 47
Bednar, David A., 139
behavior: Boyd K. Packer on gospel's effect on, 66, 114; effect of gospel on, 133–34; learning through, 162; managing classroom, 169–73
Ben-Shahar, Tal, 165

Benson, Ezra Taft: on frequent scripture study, 6; on understanding need for Atonement, 30; on Book of Mormon and Atonement, 34; on teaching methods of scriptures, 87; on example of teachers, 94; on teaching and entertainment, 97; on teaching with scriptures, 98

best, doing better than our, 9–11

Bible: teaching Atonement with, 32; Joseph Smith expands, 77–78

blessings for teachers, 104–5

Book of Mormon: teaching Atonement with, 32–34; studying gospel through, 136–39

Bradford, William R., 131

Burton, Theodore H., 10

C

Caine, John T., 46

Call, Anson Bowen Jr., 70n1

Call, Verna Passey, 70n1

Cannon, Harold, 50

carpenter, 74–75, 77

certificates, 149

CES. *See* Church Educational System

change, motivation for, 53

character, faith and, 23

"The Charted Course," 87–88

childhood: of Jesus Christ, 75–78, 81–82; robbing children of, 78–81; protecting and extending, 82–83; Christmas as celebration of, 83–84

children: influence of parents on, 145–46; making learning fun for, 146–47; learning for preschool- and elementary-aged, 148–53; learning for junior high- and high school-aged, 153–58

choices, teaching children to make, 158

Christmas: Easter contrasted with, 73–75; as celebration of childhood, 83–84

Christ with St. Joseph in the Carpenter's Shop, 72, 74–75

Church Articles, 95–96

Church Educational System (CES): importance of, 85–86; teaching method shift in, 102; prophetic visions of, 104–6

Clark, J. Reuben Jr.: on children's desire to learn gospel, 85; teaching method described by, 87–88; on teaching gospel, 89–90; on teaching basic doctrine, 92; on example of teachers, 93; on improving teaching, 96

classes for college preparation, 154–55

college: classes to prepare for, 154–55; challenge exams for, 157

colored pencils, 136–37

common sense, 158

communication: as an attribute of lifelong learner, 5–6; teaching others to learn through Holy Ghost and, 20–21; as an attribute of great teachers, 53–59

computers, 10

Index

Cook, Gene R., 113
Coontz, Stephanie, 79
courage, 3–4
covenants, teaching, 92–95
creativity in teaching, 165–66
curiosity, 5

D

daughter, Jesus Christ heals Gentile, 60
death: Joseph F. Smith mourns family members', 58–59; of Albert Jesse Smith, 67–69
de la Tour, Georges, *72*, 74–75
desire, 4
discipline: personal, 155–56; for students, 169–73
divine potential, 33–34, 38–39
doctrine: teaching, 89–92; focusing on basic, 114; effect on behavior of, 133–34; encouraging students to teach each other, 140–41
Doyle, Arthur Conan, 78
dreams, 25

E

Easter contrasted with Christmas, 73–75
Edison, Thomas, 5
education. *See* learning
elementary school, 148–53
engagement in learning, 161–66
eternal families, 67–69
exaltation, 40–41
expectations for children's education, 154

Eyring, Henry B.: on J. Reuben Clark Jr., 87–88; on teaching doctrine, 92; on teaching and entertainment, 97; on teaching love of scriptures, 97–98; on answering students' questions, 99; on shift in CES teaching method, 102; on effects of teaching with Holy Ghost, 103; on teaching youth, 104; on appreciation for gospel teachers, 104–5; on teaching with questions, 112; on teaching with Holy Ghost, 113; on standing as witness of God, 142–43; on engaging students, 172

F

fads in teaching, 96–97
faith: character and, 23; works and, 33
faithful desire, 4
Fall: teaching importance of, 30–32; using Book of Mormon to teach, 32–34; Atonement necessitated by, 38
family: doctrine on eternal, 67–69; making learning fun in, 146–47
family history work, 10
Faust, James E.: mentioned, 25; on teaching sensational doctrine, 91; on power of testimonies, 130
fear, learning in spite of, 3–4
feelings, learning through, 17
Fielding, Joseph, 45
First Presidency on mission presentations, 134
free periods, 156

G

games, 96–97, 163–64
genealogy, 10
General Authorities, 90–91
Gibson, Walter, 52
gimmicks in teaching, 96–97
goals, 11
God. *See* Heavenly Father
godhood, 33–34, 38–39
gospel: connecting points of, 134–36; teaching how to study, 136–39; learning to share, 139–40; effect of Atonement on desire to share, 141–43; creative ways to teach, 165–66. *See also* doctrine
grace, 33
"Granny Awards," 165
Grinnells, Hannah, 47

H

Hales, Robert D., 112
happiness, 97–98
Harris, Martha Ann Smith: letters of, 43–44; birth of, 46; background of, 47–48; transcription of letters of, 48–49; Joseph F. Smith as mentor and teacher for, 49–50; love of Joseph F. Smith for, 52–53; motivation and communication and, 53–59; respect of Joseph F. Smith for, 59–66; Joseph F. Smith shares gospel knowledge with, 66–69
Harris, William Jasper, 47–48, 62–66
Harrison, Benjamin, 47

Heavenly Father: learning by exercising faith in, 22–23; accepting will of, 23; love of, 36–37; standing as witness of, 141–43
high school, 80–81, 153–58
Hinckley, Gordon B., 50
Holland, Jeffrey R.: on duty to be effective teachers, 69–70; on power of teaching doctrine, 90; on teaching sensational doctrine, 91–92; on improving teaching abilities, 95–96; on teaching love of scriptures, 98; on teaching with Holy Ghost, 101; on rushing while teaching, 123
Holy Ghost: effective learning through, 16–17; responding to promptings from, 17–18; teaching others to learn through, 18–23; recording impressions given by, 23; lessons learned through, 23–25; communication methods of, 25–26; divine potential and, 39; teaching with, 101–3; teaching with questions and, 113–14; timekeeping and, 126; teaching children to listen to, 158
humility, 4–5
Hunter, Howard W.: on loyalty of students, 99–100; on blessings of gospel teachers, 104; on desire to share gospel, 142; on dealing with youth, 173
Hymowitz, Kay S., 79

"I Know That My Redeemer Lives," 161
important versus interesting, 131
improvement, 9–11, 118–19
independence, 149
institute, importance of, 85–86. *See also* Church Educational System
interesting versus important, 131
"Into, Through, and Beyond," 164
Isaac, 36–37

J

Jesus Christ: using scriptures to become like, 7–8; learning by exercising faith in, 22–23; understanding of, 39–40; suffering of, 40; as only source of salvation, 40–41; acting as witness of, 41–42; heals Gentile daughter, 60; childhood of, 75–78, 81–82; teaches through questions, 111–12
Johnson, Sextus, 46
Joseph (father of Jesus Christ), 74–75, 77
journal, 23
junior high, 153–58
justice, 25

K

Kalpakgian, Mitchell, 82–83
Keller, Helen, 51
Kimball, Alice Ann, 47
Kimball, Heber C., 47, 63
Kimball, Spencer W.: on testimonies, 26; on teaching sensational doctrine, 91; on example of teachers, 93–94; on encouraging students, 100
King, Carole Call, 43–44, 70n15
King Benjamin, 28
knowledge as attribute of great teachers, 66–69

L

Lafon, Francois, 76, 77
Lambson, Edna, 47
Lambson, Julina, 47, 58
law of teaching: overview of, 87; doctrine and, 89–92; covenants and, 92–95; Church Articles and, 95–96; gimmicks and, 96–97; scriptures and, 97–99; student-teacher relationship and, 99–101; Holy Ghost and, 101–3
Leamnson, Robert, 54
learning: eternal nature of, 1–3; improving effectiveness of, 16–17; Holy Ghost and, 16–23; making, fun, 146–47; during preschool and elementary years, 148–53; during junior high and high school years, 153–58; engagement in, 161–66. *See also* lifelong learning
Lee, Harold B.: advice of, to teachers, 90; on answering students' questions, 99; on testimonies, 132–33
letters: from Joseph F. Smith, 43–45; transcription of, 48–49
Lewis, C. S., 33
lifelong learning: attributes for, 3–6; scripture study and, 6–9;

cumulative nature of, 9–11; motherhood and, 11–12; Joseph Smith as example of, 16; for children, 147
love: Atonement as proof of, 36–37; of Heavenly Father and Jesus Christ, 40; as attribute of great teachers, 51–53; aids in learning, 149; for students, 172–73

M

Mansfield, Mike, 169
marriage: of Joseph F. Smith, 47; of Martha Ann Smith Harris, 47, 62–66
math, 152
Maxwell, Neal A.: on remembering teachers, 92–93; on example of teachers, 94–95; on importance of effective teaching, 96; on teaching with Holy Ghost, 101, 103; on teaching youth, 104; on unequal importance of information, 131; on possessing scriptures, 139
McConkie, Bruce R.: on qualifying for spiritual guidance, 18; on Atonement, 29–30; on learning from Book of Mormon, 32; on acting as witness of Jesus Christ, 41; on power of teaching doctrine, 90; on teaching with scriptures, 91; on teaching and entertainment, 97; on teaching with Holy Ghost, 102
Medved, Michael and Diane, 80–81
Melchizedek, 77–78

mercy, 25
Millet, Robert L., 30
missionary work: Joseph F. Smith and, 46–47; raised standards for, 127–28; improving seminary preparation for, 128–30; importance of testimonies in, 130; assumptions on testimonies in, 132–33; doctrine's effect on behavior and, 133–34; connecting information in, 134–36; gospel study as preparation for, 136–39; preparing and practicing for, 139–40; preparing students for, 140–41; standing as witness and, 141–43; appreciating, 143
Molen, Simpson M., 46
money stolen from Joseph F. Smith, 57
mortality, learning in, 2
mothers: lifelong learning and, 11–12; influence on small children of, 145–46
motivation, 53–59

N

Nazareth, 77
Newstrom, John, 163
numbers, 152

O

Oaks, Dallin H.: on caring of teachers, 51; mentioned, 133
obedience, forced, 26
online classes, 157
ordinances, teaching connections in, 134–36

Index

P

Packer, Boyd K.: on learning about Atonement, 6; on gospel's effect on behavior, 66, 114, 133; on seeing hand of God, 85; on institute and seminary programs, 86; on J. Reuben Clark Jr., 88; on timing for teaching, 90; on worthiness of teachers, 93; on CES teachers, 105–6; on finding testimonies, 119

pain, Jesus Christ understands, 39–40
Palmer, Parker, 60–61
parents, influence of, 145–46
Passey, Sarah Harris, 70n14
patience, 5
Pearson, Don and Ann, *148*
pedagogue, 49–50
Perry, L. Tom, 102
Petersen, Mark E., 89–90, 95
Phelps, Michael, 9
picture book, 145–46
placement tests, 156–57
pop, 170
Postman, Neil, 82
Pratt, Parley P., 45
prayer, revelation during scripture study and, 9
Preach My Gospel, 134, 137
precision in use of words, 151–53
preparation: for missionary work, 128–30; classroom discipline and, 172
preschool, 148–53
priesthood, 162–63
principles, teaching connections in, 134–36
progression: lifelong learning and, 1–3; striving for improvement and, 9–11
prophets, 90–91, 95–96, 101

Q

questions: value of, 34–36, 112–13; Jesus Christ teaches through, 111–12; developing skills for asking, 113; for teacher preparation, 113–14; searching, 114–15; analytical, 115–16; application, 116–17; encouraging student discovery through, 117–18; implementing, in teaching, 118–19; teaching with, 119–20

R

Ramsey, Jon Benet, 81
reading, 149–51
recognition, 149, 165
respect, 59–66
resurrection, 33
revelation for students, 117–18
Richards, Sarah Ellen, 47, 52
Rodgers, Washington B., 46
Romney, Marion G.: quotes J. Reuben Clark Jr., 88; on power of teacher's example, 93

S

sacrifice, Atonement and, 36–37
salvation, 40–41
Samuelson, Cecil O., 119

Satan: limited power of, 23; tempts us with good things, 24
SAT test, 156–57
Scannell, Edward, 163
Schwartz, Mary Taylor, 47
Scott, Richard G.: on gimmicks in teaching, 97; on teaching with Holy Ghost, 102–3; on appreciation for gospel teachers, 105
scriptures: lifelong learning and, 6–9; teaching method in, 87; Bruce R. McConkie on teaching with, 91; teaching love of, 97–99; Neal A. Maxwell on teaching with, 101; searching for answers in, 114–15; considering time when teaching, 124; studying gospel through, 136–39; "Granny Awards" for, 165
searching questions, 114–15
seed, 41–42
self-discipline, 155–56
seminary: importance of, 85–86; as mission preparation, 128–30; important versus interesting information in, 131; making assumptions in, 132–33; connecting information in, 134–36; encouraging student teaching in, 140–41; "Granny Awards" given in, 165; classroom behavior and, 169–73. *See also* Church Educational System
sensational, 91–92
Sherlock Holmes (fictional character), 78
Silver Blaze, 78

Smith, Albert Jesse, 67–69, 71n34
Smith, Hyrum and Mary Fielding, 43, 45–46, 49, 54–55
Smith, Hyrum (son of Martha Ann Smith Harris), 51–52
Smith, John, 47, 62–63, 71n30
Smith, Joseph: as example of lifelong learning, 16; incarceration of, 45–46; death of, 46; as natural teacher, 50; expands and corrects Bible, 77–78; on Church Articles, 95; teaches with questions, 119–20; on faith and action, 162
Smith, Joseph F.: letters from, 43–45; background of, 45–47; transcription of letters of, 48–49; as mentor and teacher, 49–50, 69–70; love for sister of, 52–53; as example of motivation and communication, 53–59; respect for sister of, 59–66; gospel knowledge of, 66–69; on seeing hand of God, 85
Smith, Levira, 47
Smith, Mercy Josephine, 58
Smith, Samuel H., 47
Smith, Silas S., 46
Smoot, Emily Harris, 47–48
Snow, Lorenzo, 47, 52
The Son of a Carpenter, 76, 77
speaking, teaching precision in, 151–53
Spiers, George, 46
Spirit. *See* Holy Ghost
stolen money, 57

Index

students: appropriate relationship between teachers and, 99–101; using questions to teach, 112–13; inciting revelation for, 117–18; encouraging interaction amongst, 118–19, 140–41; timing responsibilities of, 124; teaching important information to, 131; making assumptions on, 132–33; connecting information for, 134–36; engaging, 161–66; managing behavior of, 169–73
study skills, 155–56
suffering, 40
Sullivan, Anne Mansfield, 51
summer break, 152–53, 157–58
Super Saturday, 171–72

T
"tap lightly," 169
Taylor, John, 47, 69–70
teachers: attributes of great, 5–6, 50–51; can teach others to learn from Holy Ghost, 16–23; Joseph F. Smith as, 49–50, 69–70; love as attribute of great, 51–53; motivation and communication as attributes of great, 53–59; respect as attribute of great, 59–66; knowledge as attribute of great, 66–69; example and worthiness of, 92–95; appropriate relationship between students and, 99–101; blessings for, 104–5; prophetic visions for, 104–6; preparation questions for, 113–14; improvement tips for, 118–19; timing responsibilities of, 123–25; timekeeping tips for, 125–26; encouraging children as, 152; creativity of, 165–66
teaching. *See* law of teaching
technology, 10
temple, 75–76
testimony: Spencer W. Kimball on, 26; of Atonement, 41–42; Boyd K. Packer on finding, 119; missionary work and, 130; making assumptions on, 132–33
tests, 156–57
Thompson, Mercy Fielding, 47
time: teachers' responsibilities to, 123–25; students' responsibilities to, 124; tips for keeping, 125–26
tithing, 92
Tour, Georges de la, *72*, 74–75
trials, 57–59
Tuttle, A. Theodore: on loving students, 100; on prophets as teachers, 101

U
university: classes to prepare for, 154–55; challenge exams for, 157

W
weakness, Jesus Christ understands, 39–40
Whitney, Orson, 46
will of God, accepting, 23
wisdom, 12
witness, standing as, 141–43

words, teaching precision with, 151–53
worthiness, 92–95
writing skills, 153–54

Y

Young, Brigham: on lifelong learning, 1; on learning in mortality, 2; calls Joseph F. Smith to Pacific Isles, 46; calls Joseph F. Smith as Apostle, 47; William Jasper Harris serves as bodyguard for, 48
Young, John, 46
youth, prophetic visions for teaching, 104–6